GRAMMA LARSON REMEMBERS

The Lost Village of Rockland

Enjoy Gramma's Village

Rey Wilf

Helen O. Larson

John R. Hess is pictured here with his camera. He was hired by the Providence Water Supply Board to photograph all structures, located in the condemned area of the new proposed Scituate Reservoir, before they were dismantled. The results of his fabulous work are displayed in the following pages. His work can also be seen throughout the pages of Wolf's previous books; *The Lost Villages of Scituate, The Scituate Reservoir,* and chapter one of *Foster.* (Courtesy of John R. Hess III.)

On the cover: This is a photograph of Helen O. Francis-Wolf-Larson. It was taken on the family farm in 1918. She was about eight years old at the time. (Author's collection.)

GRAMMA LARSON REMEMBERS

The Lost Village
of Rockland

Raymond A. Wolf

Poems and Tales by
Helen O. Larson

W O L F
PUBLISHING

Published by Wolf Publishing
Hope, Rhode Island

Printed in the United States of America

For all general information:
E-mail theewolf@cox.net

For orders:

Visit us on the Internet at www.raywolfbooks.com

*To my mom, Helen O. Larson and all of the families
who lost their homes for the construction of the
Scituate Reservoir*

Contents

Acknowledgments

This is the book I originally set out to publish in 2007. It is about my mom's village of Rockland. It is told by her in poetry and tales. I have included over 150 new photographs and documents with history.

I want to give a great big thank you to my daughter Ashlee for teaching me all the computer techniques to complete these books. Also for accompanying me on a candle light tour of the new Rockland Cemetery, conducted by Karen Sprague. A special thank you goes to Karen for inviting me to read my mom's poem "The Scituate Reservoir." A fellow attendee, Thomas D'Agostino enjoyed the reading and requested to use a number of my mom's poems in his book *Abandoned Villages and Ghost Towns of New England*. Thank you, Tom, for encouraging me to press on and not give up.

I cannot thank Richard Blodgett from Providence Water enough for his continuous help tracking down pictures and maps of Rockland. I also wish to thank Mark Trembley from Providence Water for being so helpful and patient with my mom while she visited the location of her homestead August 17, 1999.

I want to say thank you again to my friend Jenn Carnevale for editing my seventh book for me. I want to express my deepest gratitude to Dean Bentley, Donald Carpenter, Ruth Francis-Servant, Harry Groves, John R. Hess III, Earl Hopkins, George Newman, Lauren Ouellette, Dorothy Pogonowski, Kathy Swanson, Beverly Tirrell, Mary Thoman, and Viola Ulm, Foster Town Historian, for giving me permission to publish rare photographs and documents from their personal collections. I also wish to thank William Fredrickson, President, Scituate Preservation Society and Ernest Gifford for all of his hard work in researching the genealogy of Gramma's family tree. Thank you Ernie. My appreciation goes to my wife Ramona for understanding the countless hours I spent on the computer compiling all of the information in this book.

Unless otherwise noted all images appear courtesy of Providence Water archives.

About The Author of the Poems

Helen O. Larson

Gramma Larson often said, "I put the pen to the paper and the ink begins to flow. I could never write like this with only an eighth grade education. People always say it's a gift."

Helen O. Larson was known to friends and family as Gramma Larson. She was born Helen O. Francis October 24, 1910. She lived in the village of Rockland until the City of Providence Water condemned it to build the Scituate Reservoir.

Gramma wrote her first poem at the age of twelve on the blackboard of her school as the workers were tearing it down. Her first poem, *The Old Schoolhouse* and her last poem, *Couldn't Help Falling in Love*, written two days before she passed away are included in this book. Gramma wrote a total of 1,700 poems.

She and her family moved to the village of Hope, Rhode Island after vacating Rockland. When she finished the eighth grade she left school work behind to start working in the mill to help support the family. Her dad had already passed away at age 42.

Gramma lived through the Great Depression, prohibition, World Wars I and II, and gas rationing. She saw the automobile come of age and witnessed "78" records played on a Victrola evolve to the CD. She watched the evolution of silent movies to "talkies" and then color, the invention of television, man walk on the Moon and a president assassinated. She lived through the destruction of the "38 Hurricane" as it slammed into the state of Rhode Island. She saw the state shut down during the "Blizzard of 78". She also witnessed a beautiful Princess in her prime passing on to Heaven to meet with whom Gramma highly respected, the King of Rock and Roll.

She married Albert Wolf in 1936 and became Helen O. Wolf. They had two sons, Paul and Raymond. Later she was divorced, even later she married Ivar Larson to become Helen O. Larson. He was a wonderful husband. He passed away in 1988. Paul passed away in 1992. They were the subjects of many of her poems. She continued to live alone and write poetry until 2005. Gramma remarked a number of times, "I believe you can live to be too old".

Helen O. Wolf in the 1940's

Introduction

On April 21, 1915 a public law was approved by the General Assembly to create the City of Providence Water Supply Board. The board was given the power to condemn, by eminent domain, five villages in Rhode Island to build the Scituate Reservoir. They were: Ashland, Kent, Richmond, Rockland, and South Scituate. This totaled 14,800 acres. Because of the growth of Providence and a few extremely dry years the city was in bad need of more and clean water. Condemnation notices were sent out in December 1916 and the reservoir began storing water on November 10, 1925. The Purification Plant began operation on September 30, 1926. It now supplies water to 60 percent of Rhode Islanders.

This is a book of photographs with captions. It includes complete poems and tales by the author's mother, Helen O. Larson. She tells her story of growing up in a small New England village in the early 1900s. She writes about having to suffer the agony of seeing her village vanish. Through her poetry, she tells stories of her childhood and of the heartache she endured as each family moved away, many never to be seen again in her lifetime.

She was born in Rockland on October 24, 1910. The village was fated to be one of the five that were destroyed. The buildings were auctioned off one by one. Her friends and neighbors houses, the mill where her dad worked, the country store where she shopped for groceries for her mother, her beloved school and the church she attended every Sunday.

She tells how the bidders would buy a building and then have 30 days to tear it down and truck the lumber away. She recalls the school house, that she loved, sold for only twelve dollars. She wrote her first poem, *The Old School House,* on the blackboard as the workers were tearing it down. She was only twelve years old at the time but it was the beginning of a lifetime of writing poetry. *The Old School House* is included in this book.

The family farm was located on a hill in the watershed area of the proposed reservoir. Therefore, it was not flooded with the rising waters. Gramma was fortunate, in a way, to be able to return from time to time to visit the foundations where all the buildings of her homestead once stood.

9

Gramma Larson tells stories about the family dog Nell, her Grandpa Alonzo King who lived with them, about being a mail girl and about Christmases. She tells of deep feelings she had as a child growing up and how after more than eighty years, the heartache of leaving her village and friends never went away.

Her poems may make you smile; they may bring back memories of your own childhood and they may make you cry. You will feel you knew her farm, her friends, and neighbors when you have finished reading her poems and tales about her lost village of Rockland.

Gramma wrote until she was well into her 94th year. She wrote her last poem two days before she passed on. It is titled *Couldn't Help Falling in Love*. It does not pertain to Rockland; however, the author feels a deep passion that it should be included as her closing poem.

So, kick off your shoes, relax in your favorite chair, and take pleasure in her stories in *The Lost Village of Rockland*.

This photograph depicts the author's daughter, Ashlee Rae Wolf, celebrating her Gramma's 93rd birthday on October 24, 2003. Gramma was still living alone in the home she helped build in 1942. (Author's collection.)

10

One

The Mills of Rockland

The Village of Rockland was established when the first of three mills was erected along the Westconnaug River, a branch of the Ponaganset.

In 1812 the Rockland Mill was built for the manufacture of cotton yarn by Joshua Smith, Frank Hill and several other men. It burned down in 1854 but was rebuilt in 1856 and leased to Alanson Steere who purchased the property in 1865. He made extensive additions to the mill in 1875. Joslin Manufacturing Company bought the property on July 1, 1901.

The second mill at Rockland was originally known as Remington's Mill but later became the Red Mill. It was constructed by Peter B. and Peleg C. Remington about 1814-1815 to manufacture cotton yarn. It was located on the Westconnaug River above the Rockland Mill. It burned in 1840 and was rebuilt. Alanson Steere also purchased this property in 1865 and made extensive additions in 1871 and 1891. Joslin Manufacturing Company bought it on July 1, 1901.

A third mill, erected by Edward Remington in 1831, was known as the Remington Mill. In 1845 it was leased to Barden & Manchester for ten years at which time Mr. Remington continued to manufacture cotton cloth until the Civil War broke out. Theresa B. Joslin bought the mill on November 16, 1906.

In addition to the three mills in Rockland, other industrial, commercial, social and civic buildings were located in the village. There were five stores, one contained the post office, a wood shop and a blacksmith shop along with two schools, a Christian Church, an Advent Church and two barber shops. Rounding out the village was Keeney's Movie House and several dozen homes that were all strung out along the now Plainfield Pike, Tunk Hill Road, and the road to Ponaganset.

The Providence and Danielson Railway established their powerhouse in Rockland that operated the trolley system among the villages.

George B. Smith, in 1846, was the first to engage in the wheelwright business when he commenced business as the Carriage and Wagon Manufacturing Company.

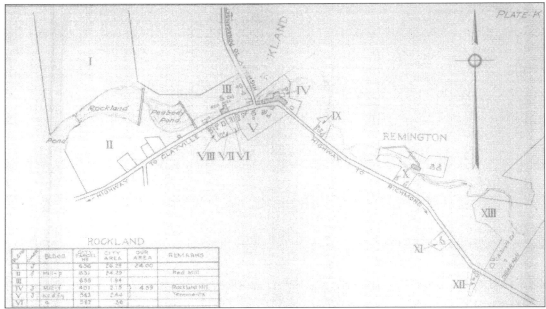

This map locates the Red Mill, number III, just north of the Highway to Clayville. The Rockland Mill, number IV, is shown on the north side of the Highway to Richmond just below the Highway to Ponaganset. Further down the Highway on the north side is the Remington Mill, number X.

This 1916 photograph shows the Rockland Pond on the left (see the facing page). It flowed into the lower Peabody Pond that powered the Red Mill. The Rockland Mill water tower can be seen beyond the Red Mill in the distance.

This photograph shows the Rockland Pond Dam as the water is flowing into the Peabody Pond. The Providence and Danielson Railway trolley tracks are visible on the opposite side of the pond. (See page 15 for orientation as they pass the mill.)

Oscar Blackmar owned this house on parcel 766. It was nestled between the Rockland to Clayville Road and the Peabody Pond. It appears to be a good distance to go to the outhouse. This view was taken January 23, 1916. It also shows the Red Mill at the bottom of the hill as the road enters the village.

This photograph displays the Red Mill on July 7, 1915. South of the mill can be seen the Rockland to Clayville Road. On the north it was bounded by the Westconnaug River which supplied power to the mill before eventually flowing into the Ponaganset River. July 1, 1901 it was acquired by Joslin Manufacturing.

This photograph shows the interior of the Red Mill, a typical cotton mill layout. This set up is similar to the mill Gramma Larson started working in at the age of fourteen to help support the family. The Red Mill was located on parcel 631.

This photograph was taken November 14, 1915. It shows typical duplexes built in the 1800s by the Rockland Red Mill owners to rent to their workers. The tracks are for the Providence and Danielson Railway as it traveled to Clayville passing the Rockland Pond seen on page 13.

This photograph is a rear view of the same two duplexes located on parcel 655. The trolley tracks and power lines have already been removed. A portion of the Red Mill can be seen to the right. At the time of demolition the entire complex was owned by the Joslin Manufacturing Company.

This is a great view of the Rockland Mill where Gramma's father worked daily. It also shows a small building in front of the mill. This was the voting booth for the area and is also seen pictured below. They both were doomed to be torn down in the not too distant future. (Both courtesy of Donald Carpenter.)

This photograph was taken November 10, 1916 from a field behind the Rockland Mill. The power house is seen to the right of the mill and also in the photograph below. The Rockland Cash Market can be seen to the far left and on page 116. A view of the barn, between the market and the mill, can also be seen on page 38.

Theresa B. Joslin bought the Remington Mill complex, on parcel 378, November 16, 1906. She transferred title to the Scituate Light and Power Company, also owned by the Joslins, on September 29, 1915. Note the little girl by the wall watching Hess. Even though notice of condemnation was given in 1916 Joslin is in the process of remodeling the mill as shown below in this 1918 photograph.

This photograph shows the results of the completely remodeled Remington Mill. It only lasted about five years before it was finally torn down and the lumber was trucked away. The foundation is now buried under water of the reservoir.

This is a view of the Remington Mill Pond Dam on November 14, 1915. This dam created the source of power to run the mill. The photograph on page 20 was taken from this bridge and shows the pond the dam created.

This photograph shows the setting of the Rockland Christian Church on parcel 390. This is where Gramma faithfully attended every Sunday as a young girl. It was nestled between the Rockland to Richmond Road and the Remington Mill Pond located behind it on parcel 386.

Chapel in the Moonlight

There's a chapel in the moonlight just down a country lane
As a child I went there in snow or rain
And the bronze bell in the belfry used to toll each night
To alert the people to come to the chapel in the moonlight
If only I had a picture I could look at today
Of the little white chapel where I used to go and pray
The little chapel in the moonlight was beautiful to see
It was just a country chapel but was so dear to me
One day it was demolished, they tore it apart
But memories keep coming back, causing pain in my heart
How the pastor would preach about Christ the King
When memories come back to me, tears to my eyes it brings
Now I can no longer go there and sing hymns
And raise my hands in praise to Him
So the chapel in the moonlight shall forever be a part of me
For there isn't any way I can erase it from my memory

Written July 20, 1991 – Age 80

The photograph of the two tenement houses above was taken November 14, 1915. They were on parcel 378 and were included with the transfer of the Remington Mill. The house on the right shows the same wall and the same little girl as in the photograph on page 18. The vacated house below is the same house as above only in the 1920's. The remodeled Remington Mill can be seen to the left in the distance.

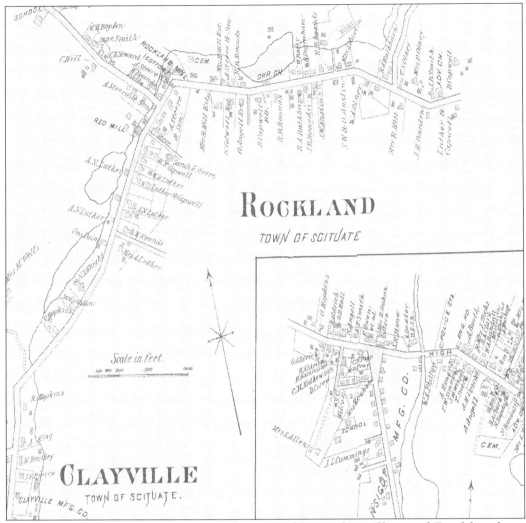

This map gives the reader a good view of how the village of Rockland was laid out along the Rockland to Clayville Road, the Rockland to Richmond Road, and the Rockland to Pontaganset Road. Most of the families relied on the mills for their existence. Life was not easy in the "good old days". Gramma tells about how Saturday was cleaning day. All of the hand made crocheted carpets would be hung on the clothesline outside. Then her mother or grandfather would beat them with an instrument, designed for this purpose, to loosen the dirt out. (See page 55.) Her older brother, Elmer, eventually took over this task. She swept the whole house while this was being done and then the rugs were brought back in. The rugs were made out of old sheets, dyed, ripped into one inch strips, and then crocheted together.

Two

The Reservoir and the Village
The Scituate Reservoir

The land was condemned the people were told
Everyone felt sorry for the folks who were old
People in Providence needed clean water to drink
The city bought five villages; people had to sign with pen and ink
Some folks were born there, some lived there for years
They just couldn't seem to shake off their tears
When a lawyer told them the city had condemned the land
They were bewildered and couldn't understand
To the scene of my childhood I returned one day
I had a lump in my throat; it was difficult to keep the tears away
As I observed each loving place, it didn't look the same
Tears filled my eyes as I passed the old country lane
I saw the road that led to a house where we children used to play
We spent many happy hours there every rainy day
I saw the root cellar still in its place
And once again tears rolled down my face
Going to the old church I walked through snow and rain
Oh! If I could only relive those days again
I saw the remains of the mill that stood in the center of town
I can't describe the heartache when they tore it down
If I close my eyes I can see them today
One by one each family moving away
Friends and neighbors moved far apart
Another family moved another broken heart
I go back now and then, the foundations are still there
I turn around and walk away, in my heart a silent prayer
We all know the reservoir has been there many years
And I still believe it was filled with the people's tears

Date Written Unknown

On April 21, 1915, Gramma Larson would have been three days shy of being 4½ years old. She did not know it, but her world would never be the same. The following excerpt is reprinted, with permission of Gilbert "Gil" Matterson's Great-grandson, George Matteson, from a newspaper article by his father May 1, 1975.

It Happened in Scituate
by George E. Matteson

It was in the springtime of 1915. Except for a few bad snow storms most everyone in Scituate had wintered well. Brakes were being picked on the hillsides and cow chips along the brooks. The robins had arrived early and were making their nests. Farmers were out plowing fields and their wives were doing spring-cleaning. Lovers were taking long strolls down by the river. Whip-o-wills could be heard calling those spring evenings. Even the cattle and horses seemed pleased to get the new fresh green grass. Yes, April 21, 1915 in Scituate, Rhode Is. was a nice place to live.

On that morning Helen Hopkins, who lived in the village of Ashland, awoke early to the barking of Bill Taylors hound dog. She had a dream during the night that as she looked up Sheldon Mountain near the east end of the village she saw the most beautiful fields full of horses, sheep, and cattle and all the stone walls were covered in roses.

Early that same morning, down in the village of Kent, Ardelle Hopkins and Frank Knight were loading ten-quart cans of rich creamy milk onto a two-horse drawn wagon to deliver to Providence.

Down in Hope the mail train had just came in and Everett Leach was getting his mail wagon ready for the long twenty-five mile rural delivery that he covered six days a week.

Up in Potterville, Horace King was planning to work in his apple orchard in back of Potterville School. And Sam Potter, with a big cigar in his mouth, was hitching up one of his horses to go for an early morning buggy ride up Nipmuc Road to the McComsky farm.

Over at the Providence and Danielson power house and car barn in Rockland, Frank Phillips and Fred Henry were getting their electric cars out, ready to leave for Providence, RI and Danielson, Ct.

Martin Smith, up at Gleaner Chapel Road, was looking in his old desk for some mortgage papers he had to sign that day.

Old William Royal Page was driving his little black horse, hitched to a concord buggy, down past the brass ball tavern and battey meeting house on his way to Olneyville to shop at San Souci's/Smith Drug Store.

Yes, April 21, 1915 was a beautiful spring day in Scituate, R.I.

And Then It Happened

Shortly after 4:00pm that afternoon Harriet and Preston Potter had just came down from Potterville with a load of wooden bobbins to ship out on the electric freight car, walked into Fred Jacques store in Richmond village. Just about that time the bell on the old crank type telephone rang. Fred Jacques was busy drawing some molasses for Gil Matteson from a large barrel in the back room. He left the molasses running and went and took the receiver off the hook. It was his daughter Vera calling. It sounded to Fred as though she was in tears. Lon Salisbury was standing near Fred and he saw Fred turn white.

Archie Fecteau, Todd Barnes, Seth Rounds, Byron Lawton, Fred Potter, and old Delaware Remington, who had just driven his old black and white ox hitched to a two wheel cart down to the village to pick up some supplies, and several young boys, including young Henry Phillips, still wearing his two buckle felt boots, and young Alfred Downy, and there were several young girls who had just come into the store on their way home from Richmond School. Harry Joslin who owned most of the mills in Scituate was also there sitting on an old orange crate chewing tobacco and telling tall stories. By now you could hear a pin drop. They all looked in the direction of Fred and knew that something terrible must have happened.

The time was 4:23pm April 21, 1915. It was a clear, beautiful day. The wind was in the southwest most of the day with about an 11 mile per hour breeze on top of the field's hill that afternoon. And the message that Vera was calling her father about was that the early edition of the news had just came out in Providence and that the Rhode Island General Assembly had just passed a bill that would about wipe out the town of Scituate right off the map.

When Fred could speak he told the people now gathered around him the very sad news. The folks gathered there that afternoon just could not believe that such a thing could happen to their town. It was settled over 225 years ago along the three beautiful pure rivers; the Ponaganset, the Moswansicut, and the Pawtuxet, with their great green valleys.

However, they knew they must now begin to face the facts when just five days later, on April 26, 1915 (while Fred Jacques was still trying to clean up the molasses that had run out of that 52 gallon barrel), the new water supply board of seven members was organized.

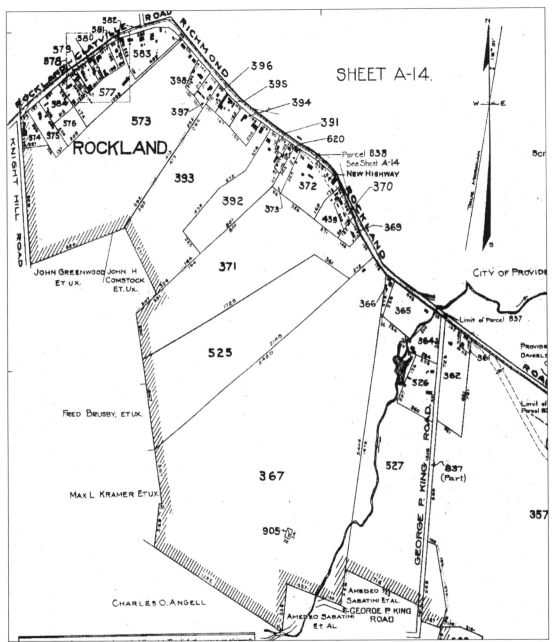

This map shows the southwest side of the Rockland to Richmond Road, now Tunk Hill Road (Route 12). Gramma's farm was located on parcel 526, on the George P. King Road. The area of the village that is now beneath the Scituate Reservoir was located on the northeast side of the Rockland to Richmond Road.

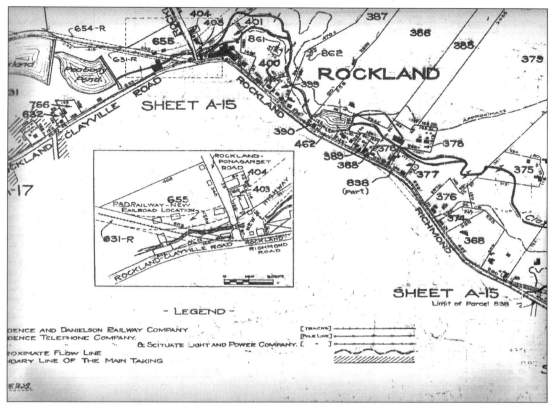

This map shows the village of Rockland on the north side of the Rockland to Clayville Road and the northeast side of the Rockland to Richmond Road. Most photographs in this book include a Parcel Number. The location of the photograph can be found using this number on the map above or the map on the opposite page. The road heading south from the Rockland to Clayville Road is Knight Hill Road. The road heading south off the Rockland to Richmond Road (facing page) is George P. King Road. The Westconnaugh River flowed from Clayville into the Rockland Pond, shown in the upper left corner, then into the Peabody Pond. This pond supplied power to the Red Mill just downstream. After the stream flowed under the Rockland to Ponaganset Road it supplied power to the Rockland Mill before flowing into the Remington Mill Pond (see parcel 462) and finally provided the power for the Remington Mill. The Westconnaugh River ended when it joined the Ponaganset River.

This was the Waterman's root cellar that Gramma wrote about on page 23. The root cellar was used before the Ice Box was invented. This was a way of keeping food cool and out of the summer heat as the earth is always in the 50 degree range. She writes about the Waterman homestead below. (Author's collection.)

The Homestead

When I was a child, I was about ten
I used to go to the homestead again and again
We used to go and get the cows each day
We had to watch them that they didn't stray
We used to go to buy an ice cream cone
Oh! The happiness I had at that homestead home
And when Christmas came, the tree in the evening light
Would make me very happy on Christmas night
Oh! That homestead of so long ago
A place where happiness lived, God willed it to be so
As long as I live, it will live with me
And it shall never be erased from my memory

Written September 3, 1999 – Age 88

Gramma's best friend, Dorothy Waterman, lived further up the lane from her farm. It appears by this photograph that the Waterman's had a very large house with a central fire place. The root cellar is located about thirty feet to the left of this foundation. Even though the Waterman homestead was high on a hill, it was taken the same as gramma's, because it was in the water shed area of the reservoir. (Author's collection.)

The Waterman Homestead

That dear old homestead of so long ago
Still holds precious memories of so long ago
My friend and I used to go and get the cows each day
With my best friend I would play all day
We used to sit out in the lawn swing at night
And talk children talk and all was alright
We would go for ice cream at the little country store
It was always delicious and made us want more
We slept in a small bed; I was always against the wall
And we couldn't have slept in it if we wasn't small
My friends' mother would make all kinds of pie
And not to eat it before bed, we really did try

Written May 13, 1999 – Age 88

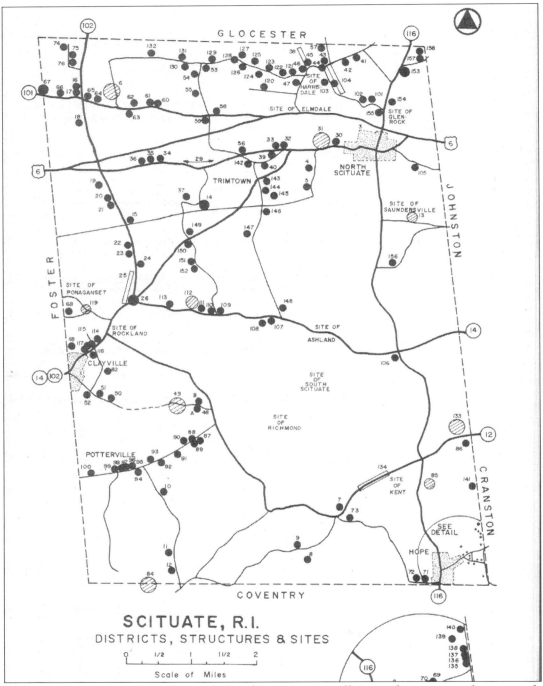

This map locates the sites of the five major villages that were destroyed: South Scituate, Ashland, Richmond, Kent, and Rockland. It also shows Saundersville, Ponaganset, Elmdale, Harrisdale, and Glenrock.

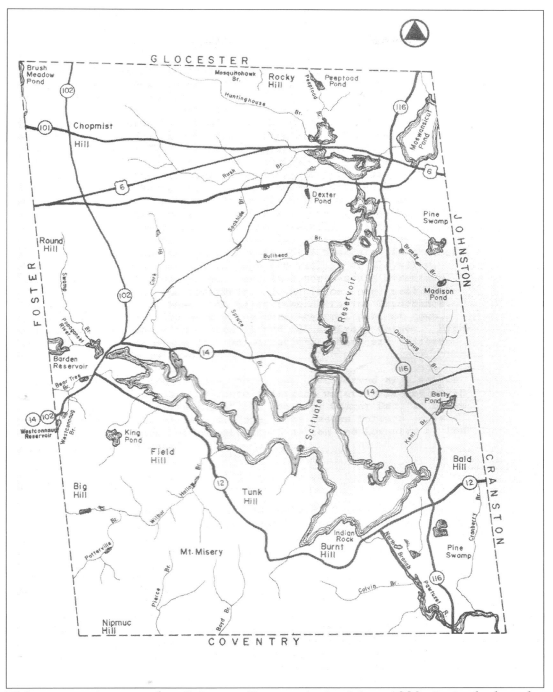

This map pictures the Scituate Reservoir in May 1980. It includes the relocated road system of today. Looking at the map on the facing page you can locate the villages.

Fred S. Hill owned this house and 22 acre farm on parcel 654. He had 783 feet of frontage on the Rockland to Ponaganset Road and it was over 900 feet deep. The Providence and Danielson Railway actually cut through his property on the way to Clayville. This photograph was taken October 23, 1916 by John R. Hess.

This photograph was taken November 14, 1915. It shows two houses on two acres, parcel 655. They were located before Fred and Leona Hill's property. The property was owned by the Joslin Manufacturing Company.

Theresa Brown owned parcel 400. It was a very small lot but included the house to the far left. Joslin Manufacturing Company owned the other two houses on parcel 399. The Providence and Danielson Railway passed right in front of them.

The house on the left is the same house as the one on the right in the photograph above. On this Sunday, January 23, 1916, the little boy sitting on the porch is keeping a watchful eye on Hess taking a picture of his house on parcel 399.

ICE STORM, FEB. 16, 1909. ROCKLAND, R.I.

This postcard of parcel 526 shows the ice storm of February 16, 1909. It happened over a year before Gramma was born. Little did anyone know that in less than six years legislation would pass that would alter their existence forever. Gramma's mother is seen on the doorstep. (Courtesy of Mary Thoman.)

The Village

One day a man from the city came to our village to say
They had bought all the buildings to be torn down and the lumber
taken away
Oh! The heartache and sorrow when they heard him say
That they were going to lose their homes some day
Some of the people were crying, they didn't know where to go
They had lived there all their lives and were heart broken that it was so
Soon the buildings were sold and the tearing down started too
And you could never know the pain unless it happened to you
One by one our neighbors moved away
Oh! When I think of that dreadful day
Oh! If only it hadn't happened and I was living there once more
Just to live in the same old house that I lived in before

Written September 8, 1999 – Age 88

Sarah F. Steere owned this lovely cottage on a 2.77 acre parcel 577 on the south side of the Rockland to Clayville Road until it was taken in the name of progress.

Both of these photographs were taken June 18, 1916. This one shows Cora L. Cole's half acre parcel 579 that was located in front of Sarah's larger homestead.

It appears on this cold day, December 4, 1916, that the Scituate Light and Power Company had packed up and moved on. The abandoned building located on the Rockland to Clayville Road was opposite the Red Mill on parcel 581.

Ada L. Warner owned this barn on parcel 364. At one time it was a working saw mill on 1.6 acres. It was adjacent to and received its power from the brook that Gramma and her brothers used to catch fish in. Warner's home is shown on the facing page.

Adah L. Warner lived on her 86 acre parcel 357. The Rockland to Richmond Road passed by her house as shown in the foreground. When the road was realigned it traveled through the middle of her farm behind her home and renamed Tunk Hill Road. She also owned the house to the left and below, on the same parcel. Warner's homestead foundations were drowned by the reservoir. These photographs were taken on May 4, 1916.

This is a photograph of the Rockland Mill and Alton Hill's barn on November 14, 1915. It was located on parcel 401 along the Rockland to Richmond Road, now recorded as Tunk Hill Road. The mill was built in 1812 and operated over 100 years. It provided a living for many Rockland families, including Gramma's.

This is a view looking south from Rockland Mill. Alton Hill's barn is on the left. It shows that all of the power lines had been removed and there was no more trolley service. Hill's home can be seen on page 54. (Courtesy of Donald Carpenter.)

This view of the first floor of the Rockland Mill shows most of the machinery had been sold and removed. The time was approaching when the building would be completely torn down. (See page 40 for further progress of the demolition.)

This photograph is looking down the length of the second floor of the Rockland Mill. It shows the progress they were making in totally emptying the building.

This is a view of the third floor of the Rockland Mill. It shows it had been stripped clean of all machinery. It just needed a little sweeping to be completely ready. After more than 100 years, the destruction of Rockland Mill was nearing.

This photograph is a perfect view of the top floor of the Rockland Mill. It had been totally stripped of all machinery and was waiting for the demolition crew.

This photograph shows the Rockland Mill was almost nothing more than a memory. The buildings on the left side of the Rockland to Richmond Road were all gone as well as Alton Hill's barn on the right. The trolley tracks had been removed along with all of the overhead power lines. The village of Rockland was nearly gone forever. (Courtesy of Donald Carpenter.)

Buildings That Were Destroyed

The Rockland Mill was destroyed, where my father worked each day
Oh! The pain and heartache to see it torn down and carried away
And the white church, where we used to pray
Was also destroyed and taken away
Then the little school house where we children used to go each day
Was also wrecked and the lumber taken away
Then the store was the next to go
Why did it all have to happen, destiny willed it so
My neighbors' houses went one at a time
And it brought heartache to this heart of mine
I go back now and then to reminisce and see
But the destruction of Rockland will forever be with me

Written August 31, 1999 – Age 88

George E. and Sarah M. Hill owned this large house on a 119 acre parcel 350. It was located on the Rockland to Richmond Road. The Ponaganset River flowed right along their property line when this photograph was taken on June 18, 1916.

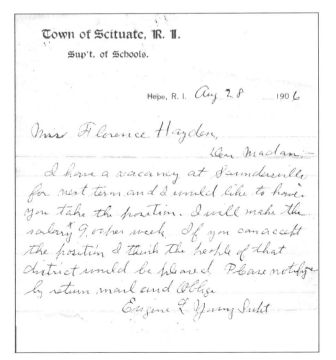

Florence L. Hill was born to George and Sarah in June 1882. This letter was sent by Eugene L. Young, Sup't of Schools for the Town of Scituate. It is dated August 28, 1906. He is asking Florence (Hill) Hayden to take a teaching position for the next term at the Saundersville School. Her salary was to be $9.00 per week. He concludes his letter by requesting a reply by return mail.

This is a view looking north on the Rockland to Richmond Road. It shows George Hill's barn on his 102 acre parcel 323. It was located on the opposite side of the road from his house (barely seen in the trees) and just a short distance from the Ponaganset River and the stone arch bridge. (Courtesy of Donald Carpenter.)

November 10, 1925 marked the beginning of filling the reservoir. This photograph, taken in January 1926, shows the three arches of the stone bridge are barely visible due to the rising waters of the new Scituate Reservoir. It was not until September 30, 1926 the system was connected to the old system in Cranston and water began flowing to Providence. (Courtesy of Donald Carpenter.)

Eliza Gallup owned this lovely home on a one acre parcel 584. It was located on the south side of the Rockland to Clayville Road. She also owned the two houses shown on the facing page.

Days Of Destruction

They were quiet New England Villages; all the houses were painted white
And as you drove by them, they were a beautiful sight
There were mills where people worked each day
Oh! The tears and heart break, when they were destroyed one day
One day surveyors came to survey the land
We were just children, what they were doing we didn't understand
When we were older, we understood what they were doing then
When the city lawyer came to buy the houses, it was never the same again
The city lawyer tried to buy one elderly man's home
He said I was born here and I'll die here, so he cut his throat and died in his bedroom alone
The auctioneer came and put up a sign for all to see
And on that fatal day something died within me
Going, going, gone, the auctioneer cried
And at that sad moment I died, I died, I died
I go back now and then to reminisce and see
But there are only foundations where the buildings used to be
People's hearts were breaking to see the striking villages shattered that day
And with tears and broken hearts, they packed up and moved away

Written January 13, 1999 – Age 88

Eliza Gallup owned three houses on three abutting parcels on the south side of the Rockland to Clayville Road. The house pictured above was on parcel 576, a one and a half acre lot. She also owned the house next door shown on page 44. The house below on parcel 575 is where she lived. These photographs taken on October 2, 1916 show how well maintained the properties were. It is not known if relatives lived in the other two houses or if she rented them.

Shady Oak Lane Rockland R.9.

This postcard was printed by Fay S. Matthewson, Photographer, Clayville, Rhode Island. It was sent to Ralph P. Nichols, Foster Centre, Rhode Island. (Courtesy of Mary Thoman.)

The Land Was Condemned

When the sun is setting and I'm all alone
My thoughts go drifting to my old Rockland home
It was many years ago that we moved away
And so often I think of that sad day
Friends and neighbors had to move too
And you could never know the heartache unless it happened to you
I went back a couple of times but it doesn't look the same
I remember the shady oak house that was down a country lane
All the buildings and the land were condemned one day
And that was the reason we had to move away
Oh! The heartache that came one day
When a family with breaking hearts, packed up and moved away

Written October 1999 – Age 88

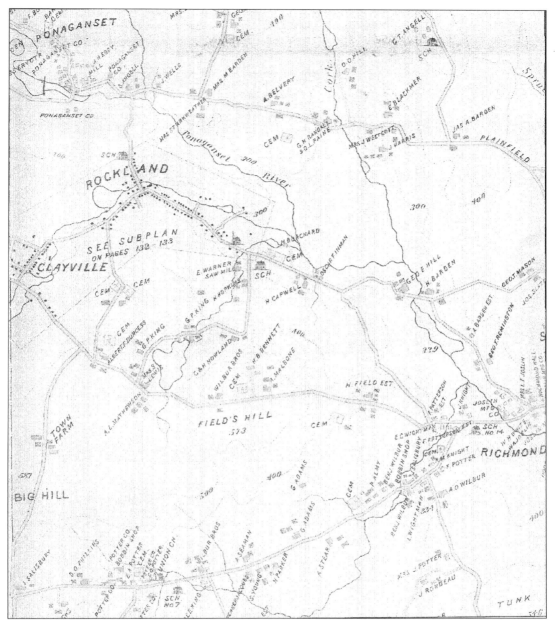

This map gives the reader a bird's eye view of the villages of Clayville, Ponaganset, and Richmond in relationship to Rockland Village. The Rockland School that Gramma attended is located near the corner of the George P. King Road on the Rockland to Richmond Road across from the cemetery. The Rockland Christian Church, where Gramma spent many a Sunday, can be seen on the right side of the road headed back to the village.

Frank A. and Carrie L. Waterman lived in this house on parcel 363 located on the Rockland to Richmond Road. The Providence and Danielson Railway tracks that led to the car barn, seen on page 72, were to the left of their home. If the tracks had not been torn up, they would now be beneath the reservoir. (Courtesy of Donald Carpenter.)

Carrie Was Her Name

If an Angel ever came to earth
Carrie was that one
And if there is a place called Heaven
There was a place reserved there when her work was done
She cared for the elderly and the children too
She had earned her rest when her life was through
She never complained about anything, she was so dear to me
She never gossiped about anyone, she always seemed to be happy
If a neighbor child needed rubbers, she would say I'll buy you a pair soon
So come back my dear child, come tomorrow at noon
If a child needed a pair of gloves and his hands were cold that day
She would tell the child stop in again today
Carrie was such a lovely lady, cheerful all the time
And I often wished that she was a relative of mine

Written December 4, 1998 – Age 88
Dedicated to Carrie Waterman

This is a view of the New Rockland Cemetery in the 1920s. Over 1,000 of the more than 1,500 graves were moved here from the five villages. The balance of graves was moved to other locations by request of descendants. Over 700 lucky souls were on high ground and left resting in peace where they were.

Scituate, R. I., *Oct 14th* 1918

Received of *Raymond A. Rathbun estate*

For **Scituate Town Tax** assessed in July 1918 $ *1.20*

For POLL Tax $

For Interest @ 12 % $

$ *1.20*

Willis J. Box   Collector.

Raymond A. Rathbun passed away April 21, 1902, see page 50. However, 16 years later on October 14, 1918, his estate needed to pay the Town of Scituate a tax that was due of $1.20. (Courtesy of Kathy Swanson.)

The old Rockland Cemetery is pictured above in 1916. Below, in 2013, is the new Rockland Cemetery showing the relocated headstone. It reads; Raymond A. Rathbun, born August 24, 1845, died April 21, 1902. He married Ella J. Barnes, born June 9, 1848, died June 13, 1923. John W. Bowen Jr. married their daughter Claribel J. on November 6, 1894. She died less than four years later, July 13, 1898 at the age of 26. Bowen married his second wife, Mary V. Aylesworth and they had one child, Mary Belle, born February 23, 1907. She passed away June 23, 1909. She was only two years and four months old. (Below author's collection.)

The photograph above shows another section of the old Rockland Cemetery in 1916. The valley seen behind it is now under water. The new Rockland Cemetery is shown below in 2013. The monument pictured records the following: Samuel Austin was born May 3, 1777, died December 30, 1863. His wife Rebeckah was born August 21, 1783, died January 12, 1873. They had three children born on the following dates; Sophia, March 20, 1810; Samuel W., June 2, 1822; and Susan M., February 1, 1827. Susan would marry Rev. William Read. (Below author's collection.)

This is a very interesting photograph John R. Hess took on May 4, 1916. First, it shows the smoke stack of the Providence and Danielson Railway power house and car barn. Second, there is a lady tending to her loved ones grave in the back portion of the old Rockland Cemetery. Finally, the large headstone in the upper right corner records John K. S. Olney almost lived to be 101 years old. It states he was born June 1813 and died May 1914, the year before the arrival of the devastating news. The photograph below was taken the same day and shows a fraction of the front of the cemetery following alongside the Rockland to Richmond Road for 840 ft.

Three

Remembering Rockland

I Left My Heart In Rockland

I left my heart in Rockland, when I moved away
And my heart is still there, today and every day
My son Raymond will take me back to the place I call home
No matter where I live, I always feel all alone
I can't forget the place, where I lived for years
And if I dwell on it very long, I may be close to tears
Yes, I want to go back and see where the old house stood
It was painted white and made of wood
I'd love to go back to that place one day
And once again see the brook where we used to play
We knew we had to move, then came the moving day
And a heart broken family, packed up and moved away

Written August 10th & 11th, 1999 – Age 88

This photograph was taken on August 30, 1916. It shows Alton J. and Mary E. Hill's home. It was on parcel 398 and contained .64 acres. They lived three houses down the road from the Rockland Market shown of page 59.

If I Could Go Back

The evening shades are falling, the Sun is going down
Tonight I'm living in the past, dreaming of my home town
The beautiful white church, where as a child I used to go
Is no longer there, destiny caused it to be so
The little one room school house, where we went each day
Was soon demolished and the lumber trucked away
The old country store where our food we used to buy
The day it was demolished many people were left to cry
The mill where my father worked was shut down too
It was also destroyed by a wrecking crew
Oh! If only I could go back and see the old town once more
Just to see the old house and once again open the door
But a reservoir had to be made; folks had to have clean water to drink
The heartache that it would cause, didn't they stop to think
But I'll go back once again and see where the old house stood
It was painted a beautiful white and was built of native wood

Date Written Unknown

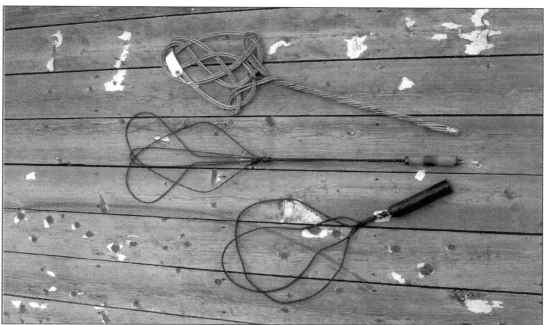

The author found these three examples of rug beaters in an antique store in New Hampshire in August 2010. The owner was kind enough to allow the him to take them outside on the deck to take this photograph. (See page 22 for details.)

Heartache In Rockland

The City of Providence bought houses, the churches, mills and stores too
All our neighbors were told to move, all of them not just a few
It was sad to see all the old people cry
It was heartbreaking to bid them goodbye
My neighbor Mrs. Waterman, a lady so kind and fair
She had to leave her home, many years she had lived there
And there was Mrs. Hopkins, nine children she had
And when she had to leave, we all felt so bad
And there was Mrs. Manchester, she loved to braid and sew
But one day as all her neighbors did, she had to pack up and go
And we realized that we also couldn't stay
So a family with hearts breaking, we packed up and moved away

Written August 23, 1999 – Age 88

This photograph shows parcel 397 where William L. Round and his family lived. It was a half acre lot on the Rockland to Richmond Road next door to the Hill's on parcel 398, see page 54, and Julia M. King on parcel 396, see page 58.

Let Me Go Back

Let me go back to the dear old farm
And let me once again see the white barn
Let me see where the home stood, it was white and handsome then
If only once I could go back and see that white house again
I wish I could see the building, where we kept our hens each day
I'd love to go back once more and see that place today
I would love to see all the red apple trees again
Please let me go back to the old farm again
Let me go back where I lived so many years ago
But the old farm isn't the same as it used to be I know
Many things have changed, the buildings are gone
Just to return again to where I was born

Written April 13, 1999 – Age 88

The old stone wall Gramma is speaking of in the poem below is to the left. From the top of this hill looking down the lane to the bottom is the Rockland to Richmond Road. On the opposite side of the road was the section of the village of Rockland that was drowned by the rising water of the Scituate Reservoir. In front of the stone wall, to the left of the tree in the foreground can be seen the top of the rock that Gramma and Ashlee are shown standing on in pages 110 and 111. This photograph was taken in 2009. (Author's collection.)

The Old Stone Wall

I stood by a wall on a hill, looking down at the valley below
A little village snuggled there neatly; it almost caused my heart to stand still
Oh! That beautiful village with the church painted white
Was a vision I'll always remember, that I saw on that moonlit night
Oh! Please let me go there once more and stand one more time
And hear the church bell ringing what a beautiful chime
The trees around all the buildings, their branches waving to and fro
I'll never again see such beauty as the village I saw down below
Just to go back once again and stand by that old stone wall
For the vision I saw that day was the most beautiful of all

Date Written Unknown

Julia M. King lived in this stately house on parcel 396 on the west side of the Rockland to Richmond Road. This photograph was taken August 30, 1916, the year she would be notified that her property was to be taken to build a reservoir.

The Place Of My Childhood

I want to go back to the place of my childhood someday
I want to see the brook where we used to play
I want to see the foundation where the house used to be
Dear God I ask you to grant this wish to me
I want to see where the coops were, where we kept our hens
Oh! I want to relive it in my heart once again
I want to see where the barn stood, where we kept our Jersey Cow
I would have to walk up a lane but I could make it some how
Please let me go back once again and see all those favorite spots today
For each day when I think of them I have to brush the tears away
Someday when the good weather comes in the spring
My son Raymond will take me there, to see all those precious things

Written December 21, 1998 – Age 88

This photograph of the Rockland Market was taken on August 30, 1916. It was located on the Rockland to Richmond Road near the center of the village. It was on parcel 573 containing 28 acres and owned by George E. Hill. See the map on page 26 for its location in the village.

This Rockland Store was owned by Joslin Manufacturing Company. Although it was facing Rockland to Clayville Road, it was at the junction of all three roads in the center of the village on parcel 583. It contained the post office Gramma would walk to for the mail. The boy on the step is watching Hess on this Sunday, November 14, 1915.

Traveling further south on the Rockland to Richmond Road you would pass this lovely home of Evelyn C. Capwell on parcel 395. It was on only a half acre lot but she loved her home and without doubt did not want to leave it.

That Dear Old House II

That dear old house in the country, I long to go back one day
Just to see where the old house stood, tears would fall and I'd brush them away
It would make me so happy to go back one more time
And relive once again those happy memories of mine
Just to see where the house stood and the barn painted white
Please let me go back someday or some night
Just to see where the hen house stood so long ago
Where childhood memories would cause the tears to flow
The day for the auction came, going, going, gone the auctioneer cried
And on that fateful day something with in me died
I go back now and then to reminisce and see
But that dear old farm is just a memory

Written November 11, 1998 – Age 88

Mary J. Round lived in this cute little cottage on almost an acre of land, recorded as parcel 394. John R. Hess seemed to be traveling south on the Rockland to Richmond Road recording history on this Wednesday, August 30, 1916.

Nursing Home

Some folks are old and forgotten and taken to a nursing home
They are kissed good bye then they're left alone
I remember days gone by when a grandpa and grammar was in the home
They were loved and cherished and never left alone
Grandpa used to tell stories of days gone by
We would listen so excited with a sparkle in each eye
Grammar would be knitting socks for a child
Rocking in her rocker on her face a smile
What has happened to some children, they want them out of the way
They say they'll have good care, what about the heartache for the home
they left one day
Don't you know you can't transplant old plants they whither up and die
Don't you know each night they say their prayers and cry

Written April 1988 – Age 77

Joseph B. Round and his wife Rena A. lived on this half acre farm recorded as parcel 391. It was a sad day when they were informed the City of Providence Water Supply Board was taking their land because they were in the watershed area of the planned reservoir. (See the map on page 26 for the location.)

House On A Hill

There was a house that sat on a hill
And in my memory I can picture that house still
We loved that house and lived there thirteen years
And the day we moved away we all had tears
There was an orchard with beautiful fruit trees
Oh! If only today I could again see these
There was a lawn with grass so green
It was one of the most beautiful farms that you've ever seen
But the house is gone and all the buildings too
There's nothing left, gone because of a wrecking crew
I go back once in a while but there's nothing to see
It's all gone now, but remains in my memory

Written September 21, 1999 – Age 88

This photograph, taken in 2009, shows the brook Gramma and her brothers used to play and fish in. It was located at the back of their farm. She reminisces about it in the following poem. (Author's collection.)

Childhood Memories

One day I walked down memory lane, old memories came back to me
We used to have a swing tied to the old maple tree
I walked through the old barn where we kept our cow
If I close my eyes I can see it now
The house has been demolished, the foundation is there yet
It brings tears to my eyes for I can't seem to forget
I walked down to the brook it was babbling away
As the water ran over the stones, so in tears I walked away
I walked back down the lane with a heavy heart
For this old farm was a special spot
I will go back some day to reminisce and see
For this place of my childhood was a special place to me

Date Written Unknown

In this postcard, mailed December 13, 1907, the view shows the Rockland to Clayville Road as it enters the village of Rockland. Dwight Keeney's store is on the left at the corner of Rockland to Ponaganset Road. It is also seen on page 86. (Courtesy of Mary Thoman.)

My Hometown

If I could go back once and visit my hometown
But it's an impossible dream for all the buildings were torn down
The buildings were demolished, the city bought them one day
To build the Scituate Reservoir, they took our beloved village away
If I could go back again and walk the old country lane
But friends and neighbors are gone so it wouldn't be the same
If I could walk just once through the snow and rain
To the church I loved, if I could only go back again
If I could wave to friends and neighbors as I used to do
Oh, how happy I would be if this could come true
Only the foundations is all that can be seen
So I will never have my most cherished dream

Written January 1988 – Age 77

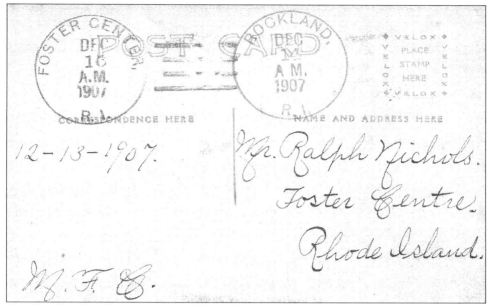

This is the back of the postcard on the opposite page. It is very interesting. First, it does not have a stamp. Second, there is no message except the date 12-13-1907. Third, it was mailed from Rockland on Saturday December 14th and arrived at Foster Centre on Monday the 16th. The sender spells Centre with "re" however; the Foster Post Office was using "er" in Center. (Courtesy of Mary Thoman.)

Down Memory Lane

I took a walk one day, my heart was filled with pain
For I strolled once again down memory lane
I saw the old tree where we once had a swing
And memories to my heart it did bring
I saw the old homestead now driftwood gray
I saw the orchard where we used to play
I saw the old barn where we kept our cow
I close my eyes I can see it now
I saw the little brook where we fished all day
And we children would cry when the fish got away
As I left the old farm I brushed the tears away
But I'll go back again to reminisce some day

Date Written Unknown

The photograph for this postcard of Walter A. Battey's general store on parcel 393 was taken by H. W. Seamans, Rockland, Rhode Island. It was mailed to Mr. Ralph P. Nichols, Foster Centre, Rhode Island on January 26, 1910. (Courtesy of Mary Thoman.)

Country Memories

We lived in the country and there were apple and pear trees
Today I am reliving those country memories
There was a white farm house and coops where we kept our hens
Oh! If only I could live once more those country memories again
There was a large barn where we kept our Jersey Cow
If I close my eyes and dream I can see it now
There also was a brook where we children used to play
Oh! Once again let me go back and live there one more day
But the city bought the land
And all the buildings too
And you could never know the heartbreak
Unless it happened to you
Yes, today I am dreaming, I'm going back in memory
And reliving once again those country memories

Written February 1, 1999 – Age 88

This receipt records W. A. Battey sent George O. Rathbun to Providence August 13, 1914. He purchased a bag of Portland cement and 28 pieces of pipe for a total of $6.95 (no tax). (Courtesy of Kathy Swanson.)

My Home In Rockland III

My home in Rockland was a house painted white
When the apple orchard was in bloom it was a beautiful sight
There was a hen house, it was painted red
There was also a wash house and a gray shed
We used to make sweet cider in a cider press then
Oh! I wish I could go back and make sweet cider again
And in the barn we had an old cow
I wish I could go back and see that place now
Oh! Let me go back just one more time
And see that dear old farm of mine
I day dream each day and make believe I'm there once more
And that I am happy as I was so many years before

Written April 5, 1999 – Age 88

George E. Hill owned this barber shop on parcel 573 located on the Rockland to Richmond Road. This was one of two barbers to make a living cutting hair and giving shaves at a time when most people cut their own.

Peter King worked in his blacksmith shop in this building owned by William L. Round on parcel 403. Kenney's Theatre is the large building to the far left. The Westconnaugh River flowed under this bridge of the Rockland to Ponaganset Road.

This receipt shows George O. Rathbun bought one Bay Horse in Providence, Rhode Island on March 3, 1914. He paid L. C. Hopkins a grand total of $200.00. It also shows he paid for it in full. (Courtesy of Kathy Swanson.)

I Want To Go Back

I called someone one day; it was nice talking to you
For when I picked up the phone I was so lonely and blue
You said you had been sick and wasn't quite well yet
You were so interesting to talk to so the phone call I'll never forget
I hope someday you call me and say a cheery hello
I'll ask you how you're feeling for I care and want to know
Please bring the pictures some day they will be so dear to my heart
For it will take me back in time to the place I loved a lot
I want to go back; I want to go back to the place I called home
But there's no way I can go back to my old home alone
Just to see the land and where the old house stood
Would make me oh so happy and my heart would feel so good
Maybe someday soon my wish will come true
And the phone will ring again and the call will come from you

Written April 1989 – Age 78

The "someone" was Frank Spencer.

The George P. King Road was known to Gramma as The Lane that she lived on. It is leading off the Rockland to Richmond Road as seen today. The familiar yellow sign to the left under the gate bar is one of hundreds surrounding the Providence Water property announcing to the public there is No Trespassing. The parcel to the left of the gate would be 362 and the one to the right was 364. (Author's collection.)

That Old Lane

Let me walk up that lane where I walked before
Oh! If only once I could walk where I walk no more
Let me once again live those memories of mine
Please let me walk there just one more time
Please let me cross the little bridge and hear the water bubbling along
Once more let me live those memories that each day I long
Let me pick the flowers as I walk along the way
Just let me go back one more day
That old country lane was so dear to me
Just one more time let it be, let it be
Let me go back and walk on that old country lane
It's so beautiful there and I want to walk there again

Written May 1, 1999 – Age 88

Gramma's house was on the right at the top of the hill. Continuing up the lane would be her friend Dorothy's house. Cross a little brook, pass the Shady Oak Tree, and end at the abandoned Shady Oak House. (Author's collection.)

I Long To Go Back

Once again I long to go back and live where I lived so long ago
My heart aches for that place more than you will ever know
Oh! Let me go back and walk up the hill some day
Let me see where the old house stood, I want to see the brook where
we children used to play
I want to see the apple trees where apples used to grow
I long to go back again more than you know
I want to see the barn that was painted white
Oh, that dear old farm was a country delight
No one will ever know how my heart aches each day
For so many years ago we had to move away
Maybe one day soon my wish will come true
And I will return to the farm I once knew

Written June 10, 1999 – Age 88

This is a view of the Providence and Danielson Railway Company's power house and car barn, situated on parcel 358. It was located behind the Rockland Cemetery (see page 52) at the edge of the village on the Rockland to Richmond Road. (Courtesy of Earl Hopkins.)

That Dear Old House

Let me go back to that dear old house far away
Let me see the old familiar places, when as a child I use to play
Let me see where the trolley cars were kept each day
Let me see them again as they go on their way
Let me see the school house where I used to go
I long to go back there again, I would cry I know
Let me go back and relive their memory
Oh! Just once more, the familiar places let me see
Let me see the foundation where the old house stood
I would be happy and I'd feel so good
I want to go back once more and just look around
And see my childhood memories and see where the house
stood on the ground

Written June 30, 1999 – Age 88

The Oregon trolley car was known as the funeral car. It is pictured here at the Rockland car barn in the early 1900s. (Courtesy of George Newman.)

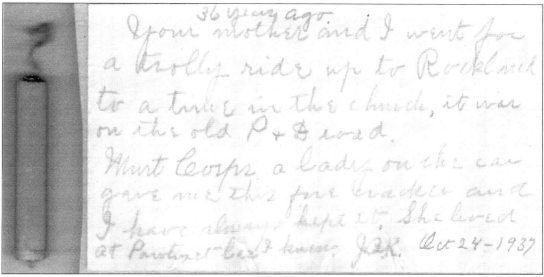

John Branford Kettelle wrote this note October 24, 1937. He explains that he and his wife, Orrie, traveled the Providence and Danielson Railway up to Rockland 36 years (1901) prior. Murt Corps, a lady on the trolley gave him this fire cracker and he kept it all these years. Lauren, his great-great-granddaughter still treasures the century old fire cracker. Trolley service had just begun in Rockland in 1901. (Courtesy of Lauren Ouellette.)

This is the barn where Gramma's dad, Andrew Francis, would paint a car from time to time. He also kept their horse and Jersey cow in there. It also contained the hay loft where Helen and her brothers used to play.

The Model T

Gramma reminisces about her father;

"To earn some extra money my father used to paint a car once in a while, in our barn (pictured above).

This one time, he had just finished painting a Model T for someone. Before he went to work at the Rockland Mill the following morning, he told us kids not to play in the hay loft because the paint was still wet from the night before.

He should never have said that, because we may never have thought of playing in the loft. But, being summer and not a lot to do, we figured he would never find out and my brothers and I had a grand old time jumping in the hay.

When my father arrived home from work and checked on the car, he couldn't believe his eyes. There was all hay seeds in the black paint that had fallen through the cracks between the floor boards in the loft, from our jumping around. It was a total disaster. Pa had to strip the paint off, all the way to the bare metal and repaint the entire car. He was not happy.

We all went behind the shed that day to meet up with the strap and the words; 'When I tell you not to do something, that's what I expect'".

This was Gramma's home on June 18, 1916 when she was five years old. The lane in the lower right corner is the George P. King Road. This photograph shows the out buildings, the well, and the swing under the maple tree. She spent many hours on it as a young girl when she was not doing chores or caring for her brothers. The farm was on parcel 526.

The Farm

The farm that we lived on long ago
Will remain in my memory that I know
I think of the white house and the barn that was there then
And often I want to return and visit there again
The house and the barn were destroyed one day
And with broken hearts we moved away
We had a nice horse, we also had a cow
If I close my eyes and dream, I can almost see them now
We had a coop where the hens used to stay
We would go there and collect the eggs each day
Oh! That farm where we lived so many years ago
Will forever remain in my memory I know

Written September 4, 1999 – Age 88

The images on pages 74 and 75 were forever embedded in Gramma's mind. Here she was explaining where the foundation of the house was and the location of the out buildings, the hen coop, and the barn she used to play in. This photograph was taken on August 17, 1999 during our visit to the remains of her homestead. The facing page shows all that is left on parcel 526. (Author's collection.)

A Friend

Gramma remembered the following story like it was yesterday:

"When we children got mad or upset with a friend, we would sing the following rhyme to the friend, *I won't let you holler down my rain barrel, I won't let you slide down my cellar door/ I won't let you play in my yard, I won't be your friend anymore.* The rain barrel was at the end of the house, where it would collect the rain water from the roof gutter. This water would be used to do the wash. If you hollered down into the barrel, it would echo back. It was fun and something to do, if we were not doing chores. The cellar door was on the outside of the house and slanted. There were no stairs inside of the house to access the basement. So again, it was fun and a pastime to slide down the cellar door. It was pretty bad if your friend could not ever play in your yard again. If it was so bad that you were about to lose a friend, an apology was in order from that friend. Of course, that is what happened and you continued to be friends."

Above is the foundation of the barn. Behind it can be seen the foundation of the chicken coop and a walk way between them. To the right of the barn foundation is where the house was. Gramma is sitting right in front of the foundation on the opposite page. Below is a better view of the chicken coop foundation and the walk way to the left leading between it and the barn foundation. (Author's collection.)

This postcard was mailed September 18, 1910. It pictures the George P. King Lane, affectionately known by locals as Shady Oak Lane. It was the lane going to Shady Oak and the old gray house. Gram writes about it and her husband, Ivar, in the following poem. (Courtesy of Kathy Swanson.)

Walking Down A Lane

We were walking down a lane it was a nice summer day
And we could smell the scent of the flowers as we walked along the way
We were holding hands and laughing all the time
That day of so long ago with that love of mine
We had to cross a bridge that was over a brook then
Oh! If only one more time I could walk there with him
We came to a foundation that once had a house of driftwood gray
Maybe someday later I'll return there one day
I go back in memory almost every day
And I long to see the places I lived before I moved away
So I'll go on dreaming of the place I loved so well
And maybe I'll go back again, no one can tell

Written July 30, 1999 – Age 88

This photograph was taken in 2009 showing the George P. King Lane. It led to the location of the little gray house. When some folks received the condemnation notice, they moved away immediately and left their house empty. (Author's collection.)

Little Gray House

There was a little gray house down a country lane
Where we children used to play every day it would rain
This little house was driftwood gray
I can still see it in my memory today
The house was empty, the family had moved away
For it was condemned to build a reservoir one day
A man from the city told us, folks needed clean water to drink
I stared in amazement at him; my childish mind couldn't take it
Then one night I looked up, I saw flames in the skies
They were burning the little gray house and tears filled my eyes
One by one the houses were torn down and taken away
And now it's gone forever the little house of driftwood gray

Written December 1986 – Age 76

This photograph shows the authors' daughter, Ashlee, by the old shady oak tree in the fall of 2009. The shady oak house Gram speaks of in the poems on the previous page, below, and the following two pages would have been to the right of the tree. The author has not been able to locate a picture of the house. Note the huge Poison Ivy vine climbing the tree to the right of Ashlee. (Author's collection.)

Dear Old House

When I was just a child many years ago
There was a dear old house where I used to go
This dear old house was beside an old oak tree
And it still lives today in my memory
The family that lived there moved, it was condemned one day
To build a reservoir we would hear the old folks say
One day they demolished it and tears ran down my eyes
And as they burned the lumber up, the flames lit up the skies
Oh! If I could go back once more and see that old house again
If just once more I could open the door and walk in

Date Written Unknown

It appears the bridge Gram speaks of in the following poem has been replaced with these logs. However, this is the location of the little bridge she remembered so well. (Author's collection.)

House Of Driftwood Gray

If you go down a lane and over a little bridge someday
You will come to the place where there was a house of driftwood gray
The house was burned down, I saw the fire one night
From a hill where I stood it was a sad sight
They were making a Reservoir and they destroyed the house that was old
It had to be removed so the old gray house was sold
I think they thought the lumber was rotted and gray
That is the reason why they destroyed it one day
I loved that old house that was at the end of a lane
And we children played there every day that it rained
I wish I had a picture of it that I could look at now and then
It would bring back memories to me again and again

Written December 22, 1998 – Age 88

This photograph was taken in the summer of 2009. It shows how beautiful the shady oak tree really is. It must have shaded the old gray house, Gramma speaks of in the following poem, all summer long. (Author's collection.)

The Shady Oak House

There once stood an old gray house down a country lane
That old house was so dear to me but I can never go there again
One day they condemned it; it was burned down and taken away
And it caused me so much sorrow for it's where we children used to play
The family that lived there moved to another town
So the City of Providence decided to burn it down
My heart aches each time when childhood memories come back to me
We will always wonder why it happened, just why it had to be
We had to cross a little bridge to get to that house each day
Oh! If only once I could go there, to the place where we used to play
We wonder why these things happen, it must have been destiny
The day they destroyed the shady oak house brought sad memories to me

Written November 19, 1998 – Age 88

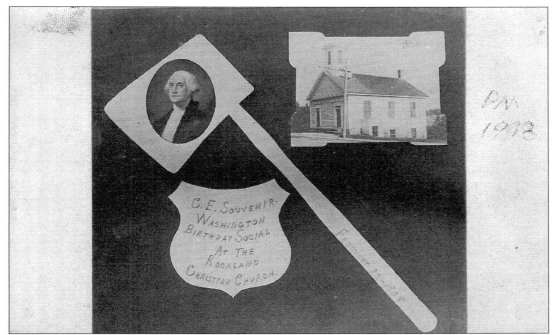

This postcard displays George Washington's picture on an ax. The ax handle records the date February 22, 1908. The crest states there will be a Washington Birthday Social at the Rockland Christian Church. (Author's collection.)

The White Church

There was a white church where I used to go
I loved that dear old church more than you'll ever know
Oh! That dear old church in the country it stood
I loved that white church made out of wood
Yes, that dear old white church by the road side
They tore it down, now the foundation the bushes hide
Some day I'll go back and see where the church stood that day
That dear old church, the church they tore down one day
Just to return to that church one more time
It would be a dream come true and happy it would make this heart of mine
Yes, I loved the white church that was in my home town
And I always went there when Sunday came around

Written June 1999 – Age 88

This postcard of the Rockland Christian Church was mailed May 16, 1917. It also shows the Providence and Danielson Railway Company trolley tracks. They are imbedded in the Rockland to Richmond Road as they pass the church on their way to the center of Rockland Village. The trolley would then travel on to Clayville and Foster Centre on their way to Danielson, Connecticut. The overhead lines powered the trolley system throughout the villages. They originated from the Rockland power house seen on page 72. (Courtesy of Kathy Swanson.)

The Old White Church

The old white church in the village, it was so dear to me
Where I used to go as a child and I was happy as could be
The bell would ring Sunday morning, it would toll so loud and clear
And we knew we must attend the church we loved so dear
You could see the people walking, going humbly on their way
Hustling off to the old white church, to sing, to kneel and pray
When the summer weather was fair and the windows were open wide
You could hear the congregation singing the old hymns inside

Written 1978 – Age 67

This postcard was mailed January 7, 1913. It shows the Rockland to Richmond Road passing in front of the Rockland Christian Church. The Rockland Mill can be seen in the distance. (Courtesy of Kathy Swanson.)

Beautiful Old Chapel

When evening shades are falling, I walk down a country lane
I sit in the shade by the chapel and live old memories again
It seems the windows are open and I can hear the organ play
It takes me back to childhood as I went there many a day
Oh! That beautiful old chapel painted a gleaming white
It looks just like a vision when the moon is shining bright
It seems I can see the people going in one by one
To pray and worship God, when the days work is done
Oh! That beautiful old chapel, forget it I can not
For it will forever be embedded in my heart
So I stand up again and slowly walk away
But I know I'll go back again to that beautiful chapel some day

Written August 2, 1991 – Age 80

The photograph above was taken in the early 1900s. Dwight Keeney's Variety Store and T. F. Lyons Barber Shop was located in this building on parcel 655. It can also be seen on page 96. Below, in the 1920s, the tracks passing the two houses on the way to Clayville have been removed, the power lines are gone, and the poles would be next. (Above courtesy of Scituate Preservation Society.)

Walking The Trail Of Tears

As I sit alone by the fire-side, memories come back of the years
That I felt so all alone as I walked the trail of tears
I would walk to church each Sunday through rain and snow
I used to wonder where God was and why it had to be so
I was only a child, it seemed no one cared for me
And from those tears and sorrows I couldn't seem to get free
My father was alcoholic, sober I seldom saw him
I used to cry and say, oh! no, not tonight again
Still when Sunday came around, I'd get dressed once more
And in a short while I'd be opening the church door
Yes, there were many days my heart was full of fears
I lived a lonely life as I walked the trail of tears
There was no one I could tell that my heart was breaking in two
So Jesus, precious Jesus, I always turned to you

Written April 16, 1993 – Age 82

Continued

I walked along with heartache all through the years
Always wondering why I had to walk the trail of tears
It seemed no one cared how lonely I could be
And as my life went on, tears became a part of me
Many times I was hurt by a sad remark or so
Why my life was full of tears I will never know
Many people are sad and they can't smile
That's the way I lived since I was a child
But each Sunday to church I would go
There I found the truest friend I'll ever know
Destiny has handed me many days of pain
But I live one day at a time though I shed tears once again
But some day I know the sun will shine for me
And then I know I will from tears be set free

Date Written Unknown

All of these men pictured here were most likely lined up for a Fourth of July or Memorial Day Parade. It is believed the gentleman third from the right is Joseph Hopkins. The tall man holding the large flag, fourth from the left, is known to be Gramma's Great-grandfather John Taylor. Folks called him Big John. (Author's collection.)

Lest We Forget

When 4th of July comes, please don't march and shout with joy
But think of the disabled veterans that went to war when but a boy
When you wave your flag of freedom, let tears fall from your eyes
For the boys who didn't come home lay in a grave beneath the skies
Think of the mothers, wives and children that were left with a broken heart
Some didn't return home because they did their part
Don't you know they faced the enemy with all the courage they had
Don't you know that many were just a lad
Many of them are paralyzed, don't you know or don't you care
They're with a broken heart, day after day just laying there
They fought for our freedom, they were the bravest of men
Please take time to visit them if you possibly can
And as you lay a wreath on their graves this day,
Don't be ashamed to shed some tears and please take a moment to pray

Written June 1986 – Age 75

The date this photograph was taken and most of the Civil War Veterans posing on this special occasion are unknown. However, it is known that the man standing tall (front row fifth from left) is John Taylor. He was born May 23, 1843. The short man beside him is Joseph M. Hopkins born March 29, 1847. They were all members of the Rockland James C. Nichols Post No. 19, chartered May 15, 1886. (Author's collection.)

The Unknown Soldier

There's a grave in Arlington where an unknown soldier lies
His name is known only to God as he sleeps beneath the skies
He went off to war so proudly, for his country he did fight
Amid the shooting and the bombing, he laid down his life one night
He was some mother's son who shed tears when he went
He left his comfortable home, he spent his nights in a tent
Maybe he was a father of a beautiful baby boy
Broken hearted when he left him, he might have been his pride and joy
And when the war was ended and the boys were coming home
He was lying in a grave which was marked unknown
So let us bow our heads this day and say a little prayer
For the soldier who lies in a grave, for only God knows who's there

Date Written Unknown

This photograph, taken January 23, 1916, shows the G.A.R. Hall and the 77 acres that comprised parcel 356. The building was originally used by the Rockland Advent Church. The Providence and Danielson Railway tracks can be seen in the foreground traveling down the Rockland to Richmond Road.

They Condemned The Land

They condemned the land and told us we'd have to move away
We were so sad and frightened on that dreadful day
We didn't know just where we could go
The city bought the land so it had to be so
Our neighbors were so sad when they were told that day
That they would have to pack up and move away
And that very day our neighbors maybe cried so they couldn't see
And that tragic day is embedded in my memory
Our neighbors moved one each day
And it was sad to see them go as they moved away
Oh! That tragic day of so long ago
It was so very sad that it had to be so

Written September 2, 1999 – Age 88

This June 18, 1916 photograph was taken from the George P. King Road. It is looking in an easterly direction. It was just below the farm where Gramma lived. Waldo L. Hawkes and his wife Alice W. lived in the house to the left. It appears from plat maps that they either sold or gave the Town of Scituate a quarter acre lot from their four acre parcel 362 to build the Rockland School. It can be seen to the right of the photograph and was located on the Rockland to Richmond Road.

My School In Rockland

Oh! That dear old school house that I went to each day
We used to whisper, the teacher got mad and after school we had to stay
I loved the children that went there they were all friends of mine
And it will stay with me for all time
I go back once in a while to see where the school house stood
I wish I could go back but it's gone for good
The school is gone now, they tore it down one day
And then picked up the boards and took them away
Oh! That dear old school house that I loved so well
I miss it so much, more than words could tell
I loved that school in Rockland, too bad it was torn down
I go back now and then to look around

Written 1999 – Age 88

This postcard of the Rockland School, on parcel 361, was taken from about the same location as the one Mr. Hess took in 1916 shown in *The Lost Villages of Scituate*, page 23. It is believed this is an earlier photograph. It appears by 1916 it had been repainted with detailed trim. (Author's collection.)

The Old School House

It was a very sad day when we were told
They were building a reservoir and our school would be sold
A man came one day, nailed up a sign for all to see
The sign read "condemned", it meant heartbreak for me
It was then we were told an auctioneer would come one day
To auction off the old school house to be torn down and taken away
Then the day arrived, the auction took place
The people began to bid, tears rolled down my face
Going, going, gone the auctioneer cried
And on that fateful day something within me died
The old school house at Rockland now is used no more
We hear no more footsteps walk across the floor
I'll come back now and then to reminisce and see
But the old school house at Rockland will be just a memory

Written 1923 - Age 12

This is the Rockland School class of 1916. Gramma is the only one identified in this photograph. She is in the front row, third from the right. *The Old School House*, is the first poem she ever wrote at the age of 12. It began a talent that would scan over eighty years of her life. (Courtesy of George Newman.)

My Seven Hundredth Poem

When I was a child, about twelve years old I would say
I wrote my first poem about my school that was destroyed one day
The auctioneer came, the school was quickly sold
It went for twelve dollars for the wood was very old
I have many, many memories of that old school house of mine
That hurt don't go away, I thought it would in time
Many of my friends went there, I miss all of them so
I don't know where they moved to, a tragedy that shouldn't have been so
I am now eighty-eight, one day I moved away
Oh! That dear old school I miss it so today
I go back now and then and see where the foundation used to be
It brings sadness to my heart, that school was so dear to me

Written March 17, 1999 – Age 88

The Town of Scituate owned parcel 420, a half acre lot housing this school. It was located on the outskirts of Rockland on the Rockland to Ponaganset Road. It can be located on the map on the facing page. It appears it is quietly waiting for the demolition crew. (Courtesy of Donald Carpenter.)

Little Red Shoes

Mommy, please buy me little red shoes that I can wear every day
I'll keep them nice and shiny when I go out to play
Mommy why can't I have them I want them so bad
If you don't have the money won't you please ask dad
When I'm playing with the children I won't scuff them in the dirt
I'll shine them so nicely if I fall down in the dirt
Just one more time I'm pleading with you
Buy me a pair of red shoes I'll keep them like new
This little child became ill one day
The doctors told her parents she'll pass away
Everyone was crying, it was so sad
For they bought the little red shoes she wanted so bad
Oh! How happy that child would have been
If she had been living and could have seen them

Written January 1987 – Age 76

About a little girl I knew as a child

94

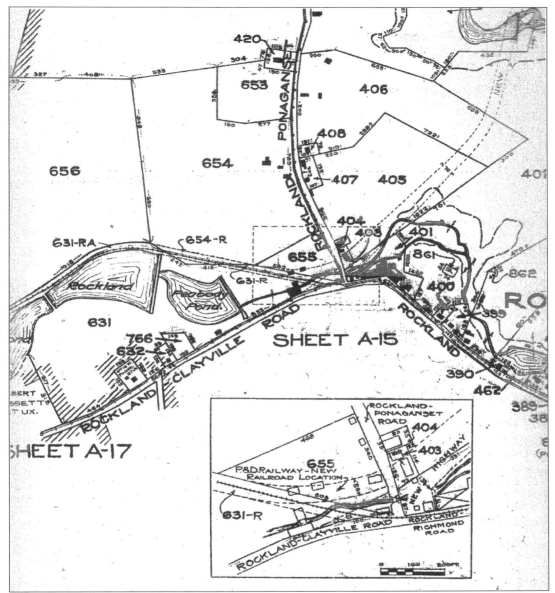

This map locates the following; Keeney's Hall and Moving Picture Theatre (page 97) on parcel 404, Ponaganset School (page 94) on parcel 420, Peter King's blacksmith shop (page 68) on parcel 403, the Red Mill (page 14) on parcel 631 along with the mills two duplexes (page 15) on parcel 655. It also locates the Rockland and Peabody Ponds (pages 12 and 13). Keeney's Store (pages 86 and 96) is seen on the corner of Rockland to Ponaganset and Rockland to Clayville Roads. Fred S. Hill's 22 acre farm (page 32) on parcel 654 is also shown.

This view shows the Rockland to Clayville Road ending in front of Keeney's store. The Rockland to Richmond Road continues in front of the Rockland Mill. The road on the left, after Keeney's, is the Rockland to Ponaganset Road. (Courtesy of Donald Carpenter.)

Keeney's Store and T. F. Lyons Barber Shop, also seen on page 86, were located on parcel 655. Keeney's Moving Picture Theatre is the building seen in the center background on the Rockland to Ponaganset Road. The trolley tracks in the foreground are headed west to Clayville.

This shows Kenney's Moving Picture Theatre on parcel 404 on the Rockland to Ponaganset Road. Leon E. Whipple owned it when it was condemned. This postcard was sent to Ralph Nichols in Foster Centre. Below is a photograph of the interior of Keeney's Hall, also known as Keeney's Moving Picture Theatre. (Above courtesy of Mary Thoman, below courtesy of George Newman.)

The Scituate Light and Power Company owned this duplex on parcel 581. It was located on the south side of the Rockland to Clayville Road. The Rockland Mill water tower and smoke stack can be seen in the distance.

Joselin Manufacturing owned this house on parcel 366. It was a small, .37 acre, pie shape lot wedged in between Ada Warner, parcel 365 (page 37) on the left, and Sarah Olney's 73 acre parcel 367 (page 124) on the right.

Four

Remembering Her Heritage

Viola Ulm, Foster Town Historian, recalls a story that was passed down from mothers to daughters over six generations:

"In the 1780s the Nipmuc Indian tribe was living in Kentuck Woods near Killingly, Connecticut. The tribe used to travel to Council Tree Woods near the intersection of Route 101 and Chopmist Hill Road in Scituate, Rhode Island. This is where the famous Council Tree was located. Various tribes from all over would travel there to pow-wow and work out any differences they may have had peacefully. Many local people in the area used to join in the pow-wow's festivities. Jeptha Hopkins and his wife Anna L. Bucklin-Hopkins was one of those families and became friendly with the tribe.

On April 15, 1787 a young Nipmuc woman gave birth to a baby boy. Her husband, among others, had passed away from a sickness plaguing the tribe. Therefore, the leader of the tribe decided to move his people away from the sickness. This young mother felt she could not properly take care of her new baby without a husband. She then remembered the Hopkins family as being good people. She proceeded to wrap her baby boy in a deerskin and placed him on the door step of the Hopkins home off Tucker Hollow Road.

She was right; Jeptha and Anna were good people. They adopted the baby and named him Jeptha Hopkins Jr. He was raised as one of the family and later married Matthewson Hopkins daughter, Olive.

Jeptha died July 21, 1854 on his farm in Foster, Rhode Island at the age of 67. He was fatally struck by lighting while pitching hay in his field."

Viola continues: "It is only in recent time that the deerskin, kept all these years, was destroyed by my brother Kenneth Walker. He felt it had been hanging around long enough."

Gramma's Nipmuc Heritage

Jeptha Hopkins b. 1753 Scituate, RI d. 1820 Foster, RI
    Married: Anna L. Bucklin b. 03 Jan 1762 Foster, RI d. about 1850 Foster
        Child: Jeptha Hopkins Jr. b. 15 Apr 1787 Ct. d. 21 Jul 1854 Foster, RI

Jeptha Hopkins Jr.
    Married: Olive Hopkins b. 10 Mar 1793 RI d. 14 Sep 1876 Foster, RI
        Child: Melissa Ann Hopkins b. 1824 Foster, RI (see page 101)

Melissa Ann Hopkins
    Married: David Burchard b. 1823 MA
        Child: Mary Ann Burchard b. 1846 RI d. 1935 RI (see page 102)

Mary Ann Burchard
    Married: John Taylor b. 23 May 1843 RI d. 29 Mar 1931 RI (see pages
        88, 89, 102 & 106)
        Child: Susan Eva Taylor b. Aug 1865 RI (see page 103)

Susan Eva Taylor
    Married: Alonzo E. King b. Feb 1854 Cranston, RI (see pages 103 & 104))
        Child: Mary Olive King b. 15 Feb 1893 Rockland, RI (see pages
    106/109)

Mary Olive King
    Married: Andrew Arthur Francis b. 05 Oct 1881 Provincetown, MA
        Child: Helen Olive Francis b. 24 Oct 1910 Rockland, RI d. 18 May
    2005 Coventry, RI (see pages 8, 10, 76, 106, 110, 130, 138, 140 -143)

Helen Olive Francis
    Married: Albert William Wolf b. 23 Apr 1906 Freetown, MA d. 21 Feb
    1980 N. Ft. Meyers, Fl
        Child: Paul Lester Wolf b. 03 Sep 1936 Providence, RI d. Aug 1992
            Watertown, NY
        Child: Raymond Arthur Wolf b. 06 Jun 1942 Providence, RI

(Research courtesy of Ernest Gifford.)

This is a photograph of a young Melissa Ann Hopkins, Gramma Larson's great-great- grandmother. Her father was the Nipmuc Indian baby left on the doorstep of Jeptha and Anna Hopkins by his young indian mother. (Courtesy of Viola Ulm.)

This photograph of Melissa Ann Hopkins-Burchard was taken in 1913. She was the second recipient to receive the Boston Post Gold-Headed Cane. It was to be passed on to the next oldest Foster town resident. Melissa passed the cane on, May 24, 1916, at the age of 92. The story of the Boston Post Cane can be read in the author's books; *Foster*, pages 121–127 and *Pawtuxet Valley Villages*, pages 120 and 121. (Courtesy of Viola Ulm.)

This photograph was taken about 1915. From left to right are (front row) the two King boys (first names unknown), and Elsie Card; (back row) Lena L. Burchard, Mary Ann Burchard-Taylor, Elmer Salisbury with his wife Mary (Elsie Card's aunt and uncle), and John Taylor. (Courtesy of Viola Ulm.)

This photograph, taken about 1918, shows from left to right (front row) Mary Salisbury and Amy Card (Elsie Card's sister) with her aunt and uncle, Ella Taylor-Baxter and Wallace Baxter; (back row) Mary Ann Burchard-Taylor, John Taylor, and Elmer Salisbury. (Courtesy of Viola Ulm.)

This photograph was taken on October 2, 1916. It pictures Elmer L. Salisbury's house on parcel 632. He lived here with his wife Mary Olive Taylor-Salisbury and their children. Mary Ann Burchard-Taylor is going to visit her sister-in-law. She is also seen in the photograph on the top of the facing page.

This photograph was taken about 1908. From left to right are Mary Olive Taylor-Salisbury, Ella Taylor-Baxter, Susan Taylor-King, Alonzo King, and their son Elmer. Elmer Salisbury is standing by the wagon. The photographer was most likely Wallace Baxter. See photograph on previous page. (Courtesy of Viola Ulm.)

MORTON,

75 Westminster St., Providence, R. I.

Alonzo E. King was born in February 1854 in Cranston, Rhode Island. The Morton Studio was owned by Hosea Q. Morton and operated in Providence, Rhode Island from 1890 thru 1891. Therefore, King would have been 36 or 37 when this photograph was taken. (Author's collection.)

The Boy Who Ran Away

My uncle ran away from home when he was only seventeen
And never once again was he ever seen
I used to see my Grandpa walk the floor and say
If I could see my boy once more I would be willing to die today
I used to see Grandpa raise his glasses and wipe a tear from his eye
And say please God, let me see him once more before I die
You see he joined the circus, but at night the lions used to roar
So he left the circus and knocked on a farmers door
He worked for the farmer, chopping wood and picking up sticks
But soon he wanted to come home for he wrote he was home sick
Grandpa received a letter; please send one hundred dollars to me
Because I want to come home all my folks to see
And if you do not send it you will never see me again
Well, Grandpa didn't have the money so his heart was filled with pain
Grandpa wrote and mailed a letter and said, I can't get a loan
So please my dear son try to hitch hike home
Grandpa wrote to the farmer since he'd had no letter from him
The farmer wrote, he had left his farm and he hadn't seen him again
It's sixty-eight years now since he ran away
I can still see Grandpa walk the floor, then sit in his rocker and rock away
Once again he would raise his glasses and wipe a tear from his eye
And say if I could only see my boy then I would be willing to die

Written 1981 – Age 71
He was my Uncle Elmer D. King, Alonzo King's son
Grandpa never saw him again

Gramma Larson wrote this note on the back of the photograph seen on the bottom of page 103: "This photograph shows Grandpa Alonzo and Grandma Susan with my Uncle Elmer King playing the flute. Uncle Elmer would be about eleven at the time. Little did Grandpa know that in six years he would never see his boy again." The author has discovered that Elmer D. King was born July 21, 1897 and died February 10, 1990 at the age of 92. He lived in Greenfield, Ohio in Highland County and passed on at the Greenfield Area Medical Center. His obituary was published in the Greenfield Daily Times. He was never married.

The location and date of the photograph above is unknown. However, the following is written on the back: From left to right are: my Uncle Elmer (Francis), me (Helen Francis), Uncle Wallie, Aunt Evie, Uncle George, my Great Aunt Mary, (your Great-great Aunt Mary), and my mother, Mary Francis. Below are John Taylor and his daughter Ella Taylor-Baxter. They are also seen on page 102. (Both author's collection.)

This is a photograph of Gramma's brother Elmer Francis. It was taken in 1916 when he was about seven years old. (Courtesy of Ruth Francis-Servant.)

Below, Gramma's brothers; Elmer (left) age 9 and John age 2 pose for the camera in 1918. They are sitting on the same rock Gramma is standing on shown on the cover. (Courtesy of Harry Groves.)

This photograph was taken about 1918. Amy Viola Taylor-Card (left) married Adelbert Earl Card. They were the parents of Elsie and Amy Card seen on page 102. She is sitting with her sister Susan Eva Taylor-King who married Alonzo E. King. Their daughter, Mary Olive King-Francis-Groves is seen on the facing page. She was Gramma Larson's mother. (Courtesy of Viola Ulm.)

My Home In Rockland II

I still dream of Rockland and all the years I lived there then
Someday I may go back to Rockland once again
Oh! When I see the foundations where my neighbors lived there one day
It causes my heart to ache because we had to move away
Mrs. Sherman would look out the window and see the people as they passed by
This woman lived alone and I often wondered if she would cry
And Mrs. Harrington lived near too, just below our home
She and her three children lived alone
Mrs. Waterman lived near to where we lived then
I wish that I could see my old neighbors again
Let me go back to that dear old place of mine
Please let me go back one more time

Written August 28, 1999 – Age 88

This photograph of Mary Olive Francis-Groves was taken on Christmas day 1958. She was born Mary Olive King on February 15, 1893 in Rockland, Rhode Island. She married Andrew A. Francis. He was born on October 5, 1881 in Provincetown, Massachusetts. They had five children; Elmer W., July 23, 1909; Helen O., October 24, 1910; Andrew A., December 8, 1913; John J., June 27, 1916; and Edward E., May 29, 1921. She later married Kenneth Groves and gave birth to Harry R. Groves on July 19, 1933. This holiday was celebrated at Gramma Larson's home on Richard Street in Hope, Rhode Island. (Author's collection.)

*Helen O. Leavies
about 8 yrs. Old*

Helen wrote the inscription above on the back of this photograph. The stone she is standing on was just to the right of her home in Rockland. This is the wall she used to hide eggs behind to take to the market on Saturdays. See page 122 for the story of the egg money. (Author's collection.)

The photograph on the facing page of Gramma, at about 8, was taken in 1918. The photograph above is the author's daughter Ashlee at age 16. She is Gramma's granddaughter and it was taken 90 years later in the fall of 2008. She is standing on the same rock. If you look at the wall to the right of Ashlee, between the trees, you can compare the large rock with the little flat rock under it, to the right in Gramma's picture. You can also compare the rocks to the left of Gramma and Ashlee as being the same. Over the years some rocks have been pushed or have fallen off the wall. Also, over the 90 year period, Mother Nature has kept piling up leaves almost burying the rock that Ashlee is standing on. Note the forest on the other side of the wall today that has replaced the apple orchard of yesteryear. This is where Gramma and her brothers used to play and collect apples for the cider press. (Author's collection.)

When Apple Trees Bloom

When apple blossoms come and apple cider too
It will bring back memories of the days I spent with you
When we were children we had a cider press
And we use to put the apples in and cider came out the best
It was many years ago in an orchard near a brook each day
On a farm in Rhode Island where we children used to play
When I think of the good times we had on that farm long ago
Memories keep coming back to me; of the place we loved so
I love to go back to that place once more
And see where we lived and loved it before
Very soon now I'll return to the old farm again
And see once more where I lived back then

Written June 16, 1999 – Age 88

My Ashlee Rae

I count the days of the week waiting for that special day
For when Sunday comes I'll see my Ashlee Rae
She's so precious and loving, that's why I love to have her near
All week long I watch and wait for my Ashlee to come here
We do fun things together; she shows me how she can write
I spend such happy times with her, she sure is a delight
She always takes her pennies from the little jewel chest
And of all the five year olds Ashlee Rae is the best
My little Ashlee Rae is so dear to me
God sent her down from Heaven to live with us you see
She's pretty as a little angel; she fills our lives with love each day
Since she came into our lives and she'll always stay
So I'll start counting the days, I'll cross them off one by one
And when Sunday comes once more we'll again have lots of fun

Written 1996 – Age 85

Five

Remembering Her Childhood

My Country Home

When the evening Sun is setting and I'm all alone
Memories take me back to my old country home
During one of my lonely days there wasn't much to do
So I got out the phone book and found the address of you
I wrote you a letter and asked if you remember when
You lived in one of the villages that was destroyed way back then
And after several weeks you appeared at my door
My letter in your hand as you knocked on the door
I knew right away that you could surely be
The boy that went to school with me
I asked you to come in and sit down a while
And we talked of years gone by, when I was just a child
Sixty-nine years had passed since those old school house days
But that old school house had stayed in our memories

Written 1992 – Age 81

Sessimon "Seth" Burnside Round is seen here relaxing and playing his fiddle in the early 1920s. He was born May 25, 1863 in Foster, Rhode Island. He is also shown in his store on the opposite page. (Courtesy of Earl Hopkins.)

Sessimon Round's wife is shown here tending her garden in the 1920s. She was born Lura Bella Cole April 27, 1870. They were married April 1, 1886 in Attleboro Massachusetts. This was 26 days shy of her sixteenth birthday. (Courtesy of Earl Hopkins.)

Seth B. Rounds takes a moment to pose for this photograph in his well stocked store. To the right of him is a bin of Uncle Sam's High Grade Roasted Coffee. Below, he poses again with his horse hitched to his delivery wagon ready to do his route. (Above courtesy of Earl Hopkins, below Scituate Preservation Society.)

This photograph shows the Rockland Cash Market located on the Rockland to Richmond Road. This was in the time of free home delivery. The store can also be seen in the photograph at the top of the next page. It is in the distance just around the bend from the Rockland Christian Church. (Courtesy of Earl Hopkins.)

Walking To The Store

Each night after school, to the store I had to go
It was a long walk and I hated it so
And I had to carry heavy bundles home
No one came with me, I was all alone
My arms used to get tired, my feet did too
I was just a child but I had this to do
I used to limp when I walked to make people think I was lame
I wanted them to feel bad for me; I used to walk in the sunshine
also in the rain
I was a tired little child but I still had to go
Each and every night I wished that I didn't have to go
Every now and then I think of those days of long ago
Every night after school to the store I had to go

Written August 30, 1999 – Age 88

This postcard was mailed December 1, 1910. It shows the Rockland to Richmond Road as it travels south out of the village towards Richmond. The Providence and Danielson Railway tracks along with the power lines that ran the trolleys can be seen passing the Rockland Christian Church. The Rockland Cash Market is the building in the distance on the right and facing page. (Courtesy of Mary Thoman.)

This postcard was signed by M.P.S. on December 1, 1910. She wrote: Dear Cousin, We are going to kill hogs tomorrow the 2nd I would like to have you and yours come down. It was addressed to Mrs. Mary E. Nichols, Howard Hill, R.I. and arrived through the Foster Centre post office December 1st. (Courtesy of Mary Thoman.)

This duplex was owned by Ella J. Rathbun when this photograph was taken on August 30, 1916. It was located on the Rockland to Richmond Road a little north of the George P. King Road where Gramma lived. The half acre lot was parcel 370 and can be located on the map on page 26.

I Walked The Dusty Roads

I used to walk the dusty roads, many miles each day
I had to go to the store for groceries and the store was far away
My brother wouldn't come home when school was out
So he didn't have to do any errands, that's what the arguments
were all about
I had to bring in wood because my brother wasn't home
I had to wheel the baby, I felt unloved and alone
Oh! Why did I have to set the table and wash the dishes
I did all I was told to do but I had many silent wishes
My childhood was filled with sorrow every day
And it is a wonder that I didn't run away
At age 14, I had to go to work in the mill, the family needed my pay
And once again I wonder why I didn't run away

Written June 30, 1999 – Age 88

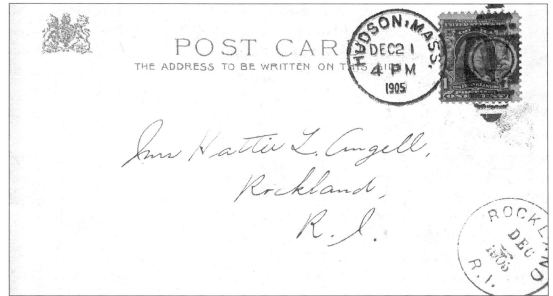

Beverly Tirrell's Great-grandmother, Hattie L. Angell, received this postcard through the Rockland Post Office located in the general store. It was mailed from Hudson, Massachusetts on Thursday December 21, 1905 at 4:00 p.m. by Hattie's sister Maude Dolan. (Courtesy of Beverly Tirrell.)

This postcard read: Rockland RI Box 78; Dear friend Hattie; This is the family and some boarders taken on the piasa. Will send the picture of the house later. I was more than pleased that the girls called on you and thank you very much for your kindness to them. I remain your friend, Mrs. Davis. (Courtesy of Dean Bentley.)

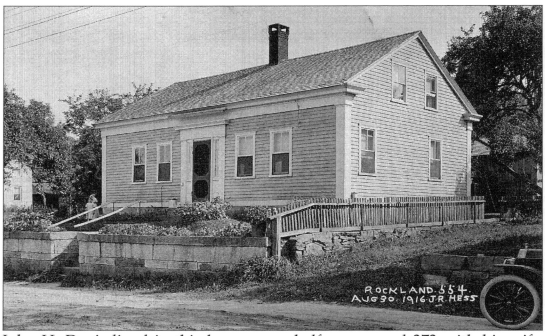

John H. Davis lived in this house on a half acre parcel 373 with his wife Hattie G. She is standing behind their only child, eight year old daughter Carrie, by the railing of the front stairs. They lived next door to Vivian Potter.

I Was A Mail Girl

I was a mail girl; I brought the mail each day
Some of the folks were elderly and a nickel they used to pay
Each day I had to go and bring groceries home
So it was easy to bring mail and I walked alone
I used to bring heavy groceries; I was the only one my mother sent
And when I arrived home she should of asked me how much I spent
My brothers wouldn't do any errands; they were all left to me
Sometimes I used to get mad yes, mad as could be
I carried heavy bundles; sometimes a kerosene can then
I was about twelve years old but I had to go again and again
Yes, every day I had to carry heavy bundles home
No one would go and help me; I had to carry them alone

Written May 13, 1999 – Age 88

Vivian M. Potter lived in this lovely house located on the Rockland to Richmond Road. Parcel 372 was a nice three acre lot. When the road was relocated it went directly across her front lawn. Vivian was one of Helen's mail customers she speaks about in the following poem. This photo was taken on August 30, 1916.

I Carried Their Mail

Many years ago in Rockland I carried the mail each night
I carried Mrs. Potters' the lady with hair so white
I carried the mail for Sgt. Potter; he was old and feeble back then
I wish I could bring back those days and carry their mail again
There was another lady named Potter too
To relive those days again is too good to be true
They were lovely old people and I loved to help them
Two ladies so kind and gentle and also one kind man
The post office was so far away, many miles I had to walk then
And each evening about five I would walk those miles again
Each one gave me a nickel; it was a lot of money then
I would really like to go back and bring their mail again

Written September 12, 1999 – Age 88

The Easter Dress

Gramma Larson remembers:

"When I was about twelve, I decided I wanted a store bought dress for Easter. You see, up until then my dresses were either hand me downs from cousins or my mother made them from 50lb chicken feed sacks. Seeing my mother could not afford to buy me one, I had to figure something out.

At the time, I collected three nickels each night for delivering the mail from the post office to some old folks in the neighborhood, but it was not adding up fast enough. I needed to come up with an idea to increase my earnings. After pondering on it for some time, I decided each day when I collected the eggs from the hen house for Grandpa; I would take one egg and hide it behind the stone wall down the lane. Then at the end of the week I would have half a dozen eggs, I never took any on Sunday. On Saturday I knew my mother always sent me to the store. I would go behind the wall, put them in my pail and take them with me.

I would explain to the grocery man my mom wanted to sell him the eggs. It was nothing unusual back then because that is what people did. In turn he would sell them to his customers. However, he said he would take the money off my mother's slip. We always had a running slip at the store. But I said, Oh! No! I explained that my father never gave my mother any money and this is all the money she would have. So she really didn't want it taken off the slip. Everyone new my father drank way too much. So the grocery man would say okay and agree to give me the change.

When I had saved enough, between the egg money and the mail money, I filled out an order form from the Montgomery Ward Catalog. Then I purchased a money order at the Post Office and mailed it out. There was one special dress I had been saving for.

The package finally arrived at the Post Office and I could hardly wait to get home to open it. When my mother saw the dress, she asked where I had got the money to buy it. I explained that I had saved all my nickels from my mail customers and finally had enough to order it. You know me ma, I don't spend my nickels. Fortunately, at the time, my mother could not count, so it sounded reasonable to her and she believed me." (See page 137 for the end).

This photograph shows the wall Gramma is referring to in the poem on the opposite page. She hid the eggs behind it six days a week until she had half a dozen, and then she would take them to the store on Saturday and cash them in. She never took any eggs on Sundays. Both of these photographs were taken in 2008. (Author's collection.)

This is a view of the foundation of the hen house where Gramma collected eggs daily for her Grandpa. She would keep one for herself, hiding it behind the wall in anticipation of her trip to the store on Saturday. (Author's collection.)

Frederick Edwin Olney was born September 16, 1876. Sarah E. King was born September 8, 1878. They married in 1894 when she was 16 years old and eventually acquired this 73 acre farm, parcel 367, pictured in 1916. The farm was located on the west side of the Rockland to Richmond Road and the homestead, a 3 acre parcel 368, was on the east side. Below Sarah E. King-Olney poses with her automobile in 1914. (Below courtesy of Granddaughter Dorothy Pogonowski.)

This is a receipt from the Scituate Town Clerk's Office granting a license to George O. Rathbun on April 22, 1912. It allows him to keep his black and white male hound until June 1, 1913. It also reminds him that it needs to be renewed in April. Lastly it was signed by the town clerk, Henry H. Potter. The only item missing is if there was a charge for the license. (Courtesy of Kathy Swanson.)

Old Nell

We had a family dog, her name was Old Nell
We loved that old hound more than words could tell
She was the only dog that was allowed in the house
She used to climb the stairs to sleep in the hallway, quiet as a mouse
One day Pa became sick and called her to his bed
That dog seemed to know every word Pa said
He said Old Nell we can never go hunting together again
So I must sell you to this man, please go hunt with him
The old hound turned around and with this man she walked away
And she left behind a heart-broken family that day
We all broke down and cried, with grief our hearts were torn
For that day a faithful family member had gone
Often I think of that dear old dog we had
When I start to remember I feel so sad

Written January 1987 – Age 76

125

Old Nell's Pups

Gramma Larson tells a story she recalls:

"I remember vividly the story of one night when my father was at the tavern, as he was every night. He was telling everyone about the litter of pups his hunting hound, Nell, had just birthed recently.

Everyone knew Andrew "Andy" Francis' hound was a very good hunting dog and her pups were highly sort after.

So when my father said he had a likely pair of pups he would be willing to sell for ten dollars, one of the men at the bar said he wanted them. My father said, 'Give me the ten dollars and follow me home and you can pick them up'. The fellow hunter agreed and they left the bar and the man followed my father home.

They walked in the house and the fellow looked at the pups in a box under the stove where they were being kept warm. He saw they were not moving. He then said, 'Andy, those pups are not moving, they are dead'. My father promptly replied, 'I never once said they were alive, I said they were a likely pair of pups'.

Pa then proceeded to take his rifle down from over the door, pointed it at the man and said, 'Now pick up your pups and get out of here before I shoot you'. The poor man did just that, he kneeled down, reluctantly picked up the box containing the dead pups and quickly fled out the door.

Remember, they both had been drinking and my father probably would have shot the guy.

Everyone was aware that when my farther was drinking, he could get real mean and ugly. Of course the following day he would not remember anything from the night before and would always be sorry for his actions.

The man may have figured it was better to take the dead pups and lose ten dollars rather than lose his life.

My brothers and I, cowered in the corner, were sure glad the man seemed to make the right decision, even though he was grumbling on the way out the door.

All of us kids scrambled off to bed and as always, in the morning, my Pa didn't remember anything that had happened the night before."

This postcard shows Andrew "Andy" Francis with old Nell lying on the family farm door step. The swing to the right is the one Gramma reminisces about in the poem on page 29. She writes about the well, pictured on the left, in the poem on page 55. (Courtesy of Mary Thoman.)

There Were Five Villages

There were five villages; all the houses were painted white
And as you drove by they were a beautiful sight
One sad day they were all sold then
And you can never drive by the beautiful houses again
Only to make a reservoir they were all torn down
I go back now and then but all you can see are the foundations sinking
into the ground
Our neighbors moved one by one
Yes, the sorrow and tears had just begun
I can picture in my mind the way they were then
But you can never drive by them again
All the sorrow and heartache we had to face
For all the houses are gone now only water in their place

Written September 21, 1999 – Age 88

The Hunting Rifle

Gramma Larson remembers another story:

"One day my Pa needed money, so he decided to raffle off one of his hunting rifles. He went to the tavern in the village with the rifle to sell raffle tickets for one dollar each. Everyone knew my father, "Andy", had really good hunting rifles and bought tickets for a chance to win this great rifle. One guy really wanted the rifle so he bought a number of tickets to increase his odds of winning. My Pa said when he had sold fifty tickets he would have the drawing. It would be done at the tavern next Friday by having a young boy come in and draw the winners name out of a hat.

When his sales fell short of the goal he had set, he decided to add three fictitious names and have the drawing anyway.

Pa went to the tavern on Friday night when the place was packed and had a boy draw a name out of his hat. Yes, the youth drew one of the made up names. No one seemed to recognize the name. My Pa, quick thinker that he was, said, 'Oh, he is a friend of mine and lives in Providence. I'll bring it to him tomorrow.'

The man that had bought a number of tickets said he really wanted the gun. What would a fellow in Providence do with a rifle? The man said, 'Would it be okay Andy, if I come with you when you deliver it to see if he will sell it to me?' My Pa said sure, why not. Meet me at the trolley tomorrow being Saturday at 9.

The next Monday night Pa went to the tavern as usual, the fellow wanted to know why my Pa was not at the trolley at nine o'clock Saturday morning. Pa said he didn't say nine o'clock; he had said eight o'clock and wondered why the guy wasn't there at the trolley stop to meet him. Besides, Pa explained, his friend in Providence really wanted the gun and would not have sold it anyway, so he actually saved a trip."

"What Pa really did was, he left an hour early, took the gun to Providence and sold it at a pawn shop. So, Pa collected from the raffle and the pawn."

Six

Going Home

Going Home August 17th 1999

It was the 17th of August, Ray took me back to the place that
was once my home
Little Ashlee went with us we didn't go alone
It was so nice of Mark to show us around
The place was so much different, trees and leaves covered the ground
The foundation had dropped, the stones were every where
And it was heartbreaking to see the clutter here and there
Mark, Ray and Ashlee walked away from me
I sat in a lawn chair beneath an old oak tree
Mark was so kind, he showed them all around
He stayed with Ray and Ashlee and walked all around
So Mark, I want to thank you today
For staying with us while we visited the place where I
called home one day

Written August 18, 1999 – Age 88

Mark Trembly worked for Providence Water
and unlocked the gate for us.

Gramma is seen sitting here contemplating her childhood home as Mark Trembly from Providence Water, Ashlee and the author roamed the homestead property. (Author's collection.)

On Top Of A Hill

I lived in a house on top of a hill, that house was painted white
And the moon cast a shadow on the house at night
I went back one day to reminisce and see
The place where that house stood that was so dear to me
But the house had been torn down one day
It was gone forever, but my memories still stay
I saw the cellar hole that had sunk into the ground
While Ray and Ashlee and Mark took a walk around
While they looked around I sat in a lawn chair
It looked so different, leaves and brush scattered every where
Will I return to that place, maybe some other time
The place that was so dear to this heart of mine

Written August 21, 1999 – Age 88

This is the site that Gramma is viewing on the opposite page. It is where her home once stood. Now, just a sunken cellar hole is left of all her memories of her childhood home. (Author's collection.)

My Childhood Home

I went back yesterday to the place I once called home
Ray and Ashlee were with me I didn't go alone
Ray and Ashlee and Mark traveled all around
They must of covered most of the ground
The foundation of the house had sunk deep down
It didn't seem the same, trees had grown all around
I saw the wall that was on the side of the barn
Oh! It didn't look like the dear old farm
There was also a place where the hen house stood, it was red
And close beside it was an old gray shed
Yes, old memories came back on that August day
Finally we had looked around and Ray drove away

Written August 18, 1999 – Age 88

This small house on a quarter acre parcel 580 was owned by Joslin Manufacturing Company. The house next door on parcel 581 was owned by Scituate Light and Power Company, owned by the Joslin family. They also owned parcel 582.

The Scituate Light and Power Company owned this three acre parcel 378 when this photograph was taken on November 14, 1915. The parcel was located just south of the Remington Mill and included both tenements.

Albert E. Atwood lived on this one acre parcel 439 with his wife Mary E. and their children Elsie W. and Edward A. It was located on the west side of the Rockland to Richmond Road. His neighbor to the left was Raymond A. Rathbun.

I Went Back

I went back to the place that I called home one time
Ray and Ashlee were with me those loved ones of mine
The place had really changed it didn't look the same
As Ray drove the truck up the old country lane
I saw it had changed so much as I looked around
And large oak trees had grown from out of the ground
I couldn't see where the red hen house stood
It was a large hen house and made of wood
I didn't see the brook where we used to play
We used to catch fish there many of a day
Forever and forever in my heart it will stay
The heartbreak we had when we moved away

Written August 22, 1999 – Age 88

This postcard is of Gramma's home taken over a year before she was born. It also can be seen on pages 34, 75, and 127. It sat on top of the hill that she is writing about in the following poem. The maple tree in the front yard is weighted with ice and is hovering over the George P. King Road. (Courtesy of Mary Thoman.)

Let Me Walk That Hill Again

There's a hill in a village called Rockland that as a child I walked
many times
Oh! The heartache since I moved away from that childhood place of mine
After school was out I had to climb it then
And when I went to the store I climbed it again
It led to a white house where we lived one day
And oh the heartache when we moved away
When I went to the post office again I walked that hill
I can feel the fatigue when I walked it still
Oh! Let me go back again and walk it once more
It will bring back memories of when I walked it before
I know I can't go back to that hill of long ago
No, I'll never go back to that hill for destiny has made it so

Written August 23, 1999 – Age 88

This is a photograph of Joshua Smith's 2.44 acre parcel 375. It was taken on May 4, 1916. It appears he had a small bridge crossing the Clayville Brook from a pasture to his farm yard. It flowed right through the middle of his property.

I Was A Hungry Child

I was hungry as a child many nights when I went to bed
There wasn't any food in the house so I couldn't be fed
My father spent his money at the village tavern each day
So when he arrived home he had spent his pay
Oh! I remember so well when we had to go to bed
Without any supper for we hadn't been fed
I think God let it happen so I would know hunger pain
And would be able to feel it when I see pictures of hungry children on TV
again and again
I feel so bad when I see those hungry people far away
And in the evening when I say my prayers I must include them
when I pray
So when I see the pictures of a hungry child on TV
I can readily understand for it happened to me

Written August 25, 1999 – Age 88

Joseph B. Round owned this house on parcel 620 on this Wednesday afternoon, August 30, 1916. He lived here with his wife Maria and daughter Rena. The small house behind it could have been for his parents. There is also a four person rocking swing to relax on in the shade of two beautiful maple trees.

Back To Rockland

We went back to Rockland, a man showed us around
I was surprised at the litter that covered the ground
We saw the cellar hole where the white house stood then
It was so good to go back to the old place again
I saw the rock where I stood one day
I didn't break down and cry I was so happy that day
Ray, Mark and Ashlee walked all around
I couldn't walk there so I sat on a chair on the ground
Maybe someday I'll go back and reminisce again
Ray would take me there, Ashlee and I would go with him
Seventy-four years ago we left Rockland one day
And our hearts were breaking as we rode away

Written August 28, 1999 – Age 88

136

Seven

Gramma's Final Years

The Road Of Life

The years come and go
As I walk the road of life each day
Hoping to meet a kind person
That will take the loneliness away

I will walk this road only once
I'll leave foot prints along the way
I know they will be seen
As others walk this road each day

And when I reach the end of this road
I will find a peace I never knew
For when I reach the end of this road
My life on Earth will be through

Date Written Unknown

Gramma continues from page 122: "Many years later I was reminiscing one day and remembered, my Grandpa used to scratch his head and say to my mother, 'Mary, those hens aren't lying like they used to. I just can't figure it out.' Now that I think back I believe he realized what I was doing all along but never let on. My mother always said that I was Grandpa's pet."

This photograph was taken in January 1991 when Gramma was 80. It shows four generations. From left to right are: the author, Helen O. Larson, her grandson Joel J. Wolf holding his son Justin Wolf. Before Gramma passed away on May 18, 2005 she had planned everything out. She had made it clear when she was alive, she did not want a wake. Her attitude was, "If they don't come to see me when I'm alive, I don't want to see them when I'm dead." She did not want a notice placed in the local paper. She was concerned people would know her house was unoccupied and someone may break in and steal her Blue Willow Collection. Gramma had made arrangements with Brown University Medical Center to donate her body for research, so there was no funeral. All that was needed was a phone call to Brown. The author's wife, Ramona, planted a small garden beside their home. She transplanted a pine tree from Gramma's property and called it Resurrection Garden. A very private service was held. (Author's collection.)

The Gentle Giant

A knock came to my door one night, I opened it up wide
A gentle giant stood there his face lit up with pride
For holding in his arms was a baby three days old
You could see the happiness reached his very soul
It was his first baby, as cute as could be
And tears filled my eyes; it was a great-grandchild to me
He sat on the couch so tenderly he held him that night
I thought the angels must be watching such a loving precious sight
God bless this gentle giant, he's more than six feet tall you see
He's so dear to my heart because he's a grandson to me

Written December 1990 – Age 80

My Paper Family

I have so many loved ones but I can't see them each day
So I display their pictures, it helps me get through the day
Each time I look at them I know I'm lucky as can be
To have so many loved ones sending pictures to me
I call them my paper family; they smile at me when I walk by
Oh! If I didn't have them, each day I would be lonely and cry
It helps me to fill the empty place that's in my heart each day
It helps me in so many ways to pass the time away
Then every now and then they come and visit me
I shed tears of happiness for I'm happy as can be
So they sit on my hutch and smile at me each day
My loving paper family helps me pass the time away

Written November 1998 – Age 88

One of the pictures, Gramma is speaking of in this poem, can be seen on the hutch behind her on the opposite page.

This photograph was taken Christmas day 1992. It shows Granddaughter Ashlee Rae Wolf opening one of her gifts. At the time Ashlee was 18 months old, Gramma 82. (Author's collection.)

Christmas Memories

I remember Christmas at the homestead, there was so much Holiday cheer
We kept on counting the days hoping Christmas soon would be here
We would go with Uncle Frank to the woods; we would giggle and laugh with glee
As he swung his old ax cutting down the biggest tree
We would carry the tree to the house, stand it in the corner of the room
We were so very excited, Christmas couldn't come too soon
Aunt Rebecca and Aunt Eliza would sit in their rocking chairs
I can see them to this day so graceful with their silver hair
We would sit and string pop corn and also cranberries too
We were tired and sleepy children when the day was through
Aunt Carrie was busy making pies and other good foods, you know
And how we children prayed that Christmas day it would snow
At last Christmas morning arrived, the snow was on the trees
My heart still bursts with joy as I remember these Christmas memories

Written Nov. 1977 – Age 67

Another year rolled around as this photograph was taken on Christmas day 1993. Gramma was now 83 years old, living alone, crocheting, and writing poetry to pass the time of day. (Author's collection.)

Upon The Christmas Tree

When snowflakes are falling upon a Christmas tree
It takes me back to long ago when Christmas meant so much to me
It was at the homestead in a corner of the room
Stood the Christmas tree and it ended all too soon
Those days they used the horse and sleigh
Oh, if I could only go back for just one Christmas day
Stringing cranberries and pop corn, wrapping Christmas gifts too
We were tired but happy children when the day was through
So if you have children let them have a merry Christmas day
For soon they'll be grown, married and moved away
So as I watch the snowflakes silently coming down
So lightly floating as they touch the ground
Tears fill my eyes so I can hardly see
As the snowflakes fall upon the Christmas tree

Date Written Unknown

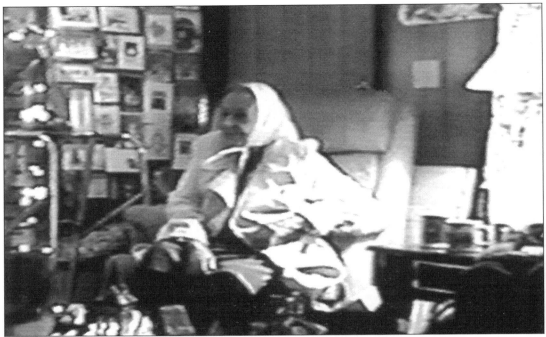

The years kept rolling by to Christmas day 2000. She is seen here celebrating the holiday at the author's home. Gramma had reached the milestone of 90 years old on October 24th. (Author's collection.)

. Does Jesus Cry On Christmas Eve

Does Jesus cry on Christmas Eve because some people forget Him
Some teach their children about Santa and not about Him
Does He cry because of all the Christmas lights
And some people forget about that first Christmas Night
Does He cry because they think about the Christmas tree
And not about Him who died to set the sinners free
Does He cry when they eat and forget to say a prayer
Don't they know He said I will always be there
Does He cry once more again
Because they forget He came to save the world from sin
Let us always remember that first Christmas Night
When Mary laid baby Jesus in a manger wrapped in swaddling
clothes of white

Written December 7, 2000 – Age 90

Eight

The End of the Story

This is a photograph of Gramma Larson giving the author a ride on his sled in 1947. They are on Jackson Flat Road in Hope. The Evergreen Inn was located on the left just behind the vehicle. A picture of the Inn can be seen in *Pawtuxet Valley Villages: Hope to Natick to Washington* on page 33. (Author's collection.)

Where to begin:

Gramma was a really remarkable woman. She had her little idiosyncrasies, like we all do, but she also had some amazing qualities and this is why we honor her memory today.

I have memories of Gramma from way back when I was a little kid. I always cherished our visits from New York to Rhode Island and being able to spend time with her. We wrote to each other frequently, even through my college years. She would tape quarters to her letters so I would have money for laundry. This was her way of helping me and a gesture that was thoughtful beyond measure.

Gramma was full of stories from her youth and what an absolutely remarkable memory. She remembered things like it was yesterday and she would tell of tales that would make you laugh, cry, or just be amused. Her quick wit and sparkling eyes had a way of capturing your attention and she could keep you occupied with her stories for hours on end.

Gramma also loved to collect things, her spectacular collections of oil lamps and blue willow dinnerware would make your jaw drop. She loved flea markets and yard sales, bargaining with the person to get a special item for an incredible price, enabling her to grow her collections. I would love taking her to yard sales, she knew the roads of Rhode Island like the back of her hands and she would direct me to every sale on her list, taking out her walker so she could go out to look at the items or if she was too tired, I was directed to bring the item to the car for her to look at. It was always an adventure.

Gramma also taught herself how to crochet, and throughout the years gifted people she loved with a beautiful afghan and matching doilies. Gramma had a giving spirit, if you wanted or needed something that she had, she would give it to you. She also made doilies and pot holders to give to people that she encounted, as a thank you or just to make them smile. It brought joy to her to be able to share with others. Especially when she shared her poems and her love of Jesus with the world around her, sending out poems to people all over the country, showing them the love and sacrifice that Jesus made for them and perhaps changing their eternal destiny.

I will miss Gramma, all the little things that we did together but I will keep in my memory how much love she shared with me, how she loved her sons, her grand-kids and great-grand-kids. How intelligent, gifted and generous she was and I will see her again in Heaven.

Your Granddaughter, Laura Lynn Wolf-Olsen

This photograph shows Laura Lynn Wolf-Olsen slowly reading her eulogy (seen on the facing page) June 5, 2005 at Gramma's Memorial Service and dedication of the Resurrection Garden. Ashlee waits patiently to play *The Old Rugged Cross* on her flute. At the conclusion of the service, Elvis sang *Amazing Grace* especially for Gramma Larson. (Author's collection.)

Resurrection Garden

I'd love to make a garden, so beautiful to see
I'd name it Resurrection Garden and in the midst I'd plant a tree
I'd stand a cross at the entrance where all around it could be seen
And when folks walked by, it would seem like a dream
I'd plant some white lilies on each and every side
As a reminder to all that Jesus Christ once died
Oh! This Resurrection Garden would be famous everywhere
And folks would ask one another have you ever walked there
I'd dedicate this garden a memorial to Him
This precious sinless lamb who died for sin
I know I can never make it but this dream is in my heart
Maybe someone will read my poem and the garden they will start
If they do, my greatest wish is, it will be where all can see
And that they will inscribe a plaque in Jesus' memory

Written September 20, 1991 – Age 80

Seen here from left to right are, the author, Gramma's brother Harry Groves with his wife Theresa, the author's wife Ramona, Gramma's Granddaughter Laura Lynn Wolf-Olsen, Ramona's mother Mona Cardente and her husband Domenic, and Ashlee Wolf. Reverend Bill Flug is in front of Gramma's garden. Her transplanted pine tree is to the right of the picture. The light the camera caught in the photograph below appears as though Gramma was watching over us while Reverend Flug read the last poem she wrote, *Couldn't Help Falling in Love*? (Both author's collection.)

Couldn't Help Falling In Love

Elvis I love you and soon we will meet
Together hand in hand we will walk God's golden street
Meet me at Heaven's gate and open it for me
Please Elvis be singing Amazing Grace for it is my favorite Hymn you see
I have lived a long time and loved you over half my years
When you sing How Great Thou Art to my eyes it brings tears
Introduce me to Jesus such a good friend he's been to me
Always there when I needed him and now will set me free
Your fans still miss but not as much as I
And soon we will be together in the sky
I am listening to your CD, what ever that is
With my son Raymond, his visits with me I will miss
My time on God's Earth is getting short
I am so happy that your records and tapes I bought
They comforted me so when my spirits were down
I would sit and listen as they went round and round
My Grandson Joel was born on January 8th
The date you were born in Tupelo, he will soon have his fourth
My son Raymond and Ramona were married on the 16th of August
Such a sad day in history, the date you were called to leave us
I cannot drink and I cannot eat
I can only lay here, can't even feel my feet
Over the years almost seventeen hundred poems I have been writing
Some of you, some of Jesus, others of my life, family and any happenings
As I go to sleep and this poem closes my book to you
I will be dreaming of meeting my love Ivar, my son Paul, Jesus and you too

Good Night Elvis

Written May 16, 2005
Age 94 yrs. – 6 mos. – 25 days
October 24, 1910 – May 18, 2005

Gramma Larson has left the building

The author and his mother hope you have enjoyed
The Lost Village of Rockland

About the Author

Raymond A. Wolf

Raymond A. Wolf is Helen O. "Gramma" Larson's son. He had felt strongly for a number of years that her poetry should be in book form. Therefore, he has put together this book of her poems and tales along with photographs, documents, and history of Rockland in tribute to her. His only regret is that he had not published this book years ago so she could have enjoyed it also.

Gramma, after eighty years, never got over the condemnation of her beloved village of Rockland or of her neighbors moving away, one at a time, many never to be seen again in her lifetime. You will feel in her writings how it left a deep emotional wound that she just could not heal.

Wolf is a native of Scituate, living in the village of Hope with his wife Ramona, daughter Ashlee Rae, and Zoey the cat.

If you enjoyed her poems in this book, you would also enjoy the author's previous books; *The Lost Villages of Scituate, The Scituate Reservoir, Foster, West Warwick, Pawtuxet Valley Villages: Hope to Natick to Washington, and Coventry.* (See page 150.) They all include one of Gramma's complete poems in the introduction, with verses of her other poems sprinkled throughout the pages.

He has made many contacts and collected over 150 new photographs and documents to bring this book to life. This is the original book he tried to publish in 2007. Finally, *The Lost Village of Rockland* is in your hands.

Index of Poems

To order Ray's previous books visit:
www.raywolfbooks.com

The Lost Villages of Scituate: In 1915, the general assembly appointed the Providence Water Supply Board to condemn 14,800 acres of land in rural Scituate. The hardworking people of the five villages were devastated. By December 1916, notices were delivered to the villagers stating that the homes and land they had owned for generations were....

The Scituate Reservoir In 1772, portions of Providence received water through a system of hollowed out logs. By 1869 the public voted in favor of introducing water into the city from the Pawtuxet River in Cranston. By 1900, it was clear more, and purer water was needed. A public law was approved on April 21, 1915, creating the Providence Water Supply

West Warwick: By 1912, the citizens of the western portion of Warwick had been talking about secession. They possessed all the mills on the Pawtuxet River and were largely democratic, while the eastern section was primarily republican. Finally in 1913, the town of West Warwick was incorporated and became the youngest town in the state of Rhode

Foster Originally incorporated as part of Scituate in 1731, became a separate community in 1781. The town was named in honor of Theodore Foster, a coauthor of the bill of incorporation. By 1820, the population topped out at 2,900 and then sharply declined. The population would not surpass the 1820 figures until 1975,

Pawtuxet Valley Villages: Between 1806 and 1821, a dozen mills were built on the Pawtuxet River, shaping the economy of surrounding villages. The mills provided a livelihood for the villagers who settled in the valley and drew immigrants looking for a better life from Canada, Italy, Portugal, Sweden, and other faraway countries.

Coventry On August 21, 1741, the area west of what is now the town of West Warwick was incorporated into the Township of Coventry. The railroad would traverse Coventry in the mid-1800s, providing the gristmills, sawmills, and farmers with a quicker way to send their goods to market and to receive supplies in return.